A Portrait of Osun
A Yoruba Goddess in Osogbo and the Americas

Adewale Kuyebi, PhD

Acknowledgements

All glory and honor to Jesus Christ, my Lord and Savior, for the outcome of this project. He is the one who has exposed every work of darkness, and made it that the Truth of the gospel may be known throughout the world. From my heart I say thank you to the members of my doctoral committee and the examiners, most especially Prof. Egil Grislis. He encouraged me throughout the program. I am proud to be your student. I appreciate Prof. Dawne McCance, the Head of the Department of Religion at the University of Manitoba. Thank you for giving me the first opportunity to teach at the university level for three years. Prof. Eduard Schludermann offered useful insights during my research. At one point, he offered me one of his offices to do my research. God bless you. Prof. Irvin Hexham from the University of Calgary, my external examiner, thank you for all your positive comments.

I say thank you to my early mentors: Rev (Dr) Samuel K. Abiara, Rev (Dr) Olushola Odelami, Pastor Gbade Oyewole, and Rev (Dr) Andrew D. McRae for your spiritual and academic guidance. Thanks to the members and ministers of the Christ Apostolic Church, Agbala-Itura Worldwide. My friends in the Christian ministries that deserve special appreciations are: Pastors Z. O. Oloba, David Adenodi, Tokunbo Okunnu, Sunday Orogun and Dr. Emmanuel Tukasi. Thanks to my best-friend, my wife, Lady Evangelist Florence Aderonke Kuyebi and our delightful children Gloria, Samuel, Deborah, Abigail, Sarah and Hannah, you are wonderful children!

I am grateful for the time and encouragement of my editorial friends and colleagues in the Lord: Prof. Wole Akinremi, Pastor Peter Kuku, Mr. Tunji Olaleye, Ms. Barbara McDonnell, Rev (Dr) Amos Adeniyi, Evang. Remi Adelugba, Dr. Bode Osobu, Dr. Julius Komolafe, Mrs Abigail Adelabu, and Elder Femi Akinwale. As you read the paper, your comments and criticisms encouraged me to finish this dissertation. Thanks to Mr. Chinedu Onyejelem, the founder of Metro Eireann Publications which provided the initial funds for the publication of this project.

My parents deserve sincere thanks: Chief Saula Adisa Kuyebi and Deaconess Ruth Kuyebi. Again, I say thank you to my wife, Evangelist Florence Aderonke Kuyebi.

Dedication

This book is dedicated to our Lord and Savior Jesus Christ and to all His children around the world, most especially my wife Evangelist Aderonke Florence Kuyebi and our children, our Christian friends and families at the Passion for Souls Christian Ministries in Nigeria, Universal Gospel Apostolic Church in Nigeria, Acadia Divinity College in Canada, Christ Memorial Church in Holland Michigan, and Christ Apostolic Church Worldwide. This work is just an academic exercise. I believe in the Holy Bible, especially Ephesians 5, verses 8-14,

[8] "For you were once darkness, but now you are light in the Lord. Live as children of light [9] (for the fruit of the light consists in all goodness, righteousness and truth) [10] and find out what pleases the Lord. [11] Have nothing to do with the fruitless deeds of darkness, but rather expose them. [12] For it is shameful even to mention what the disobedient do in secret. [13] But everything exposed by the light becomes visible, [14] for it is light that makes everything visible. This is why it is said: "Wake up, O sleeper, rise from the dead, and Christ will shine on you."

(NKJV)

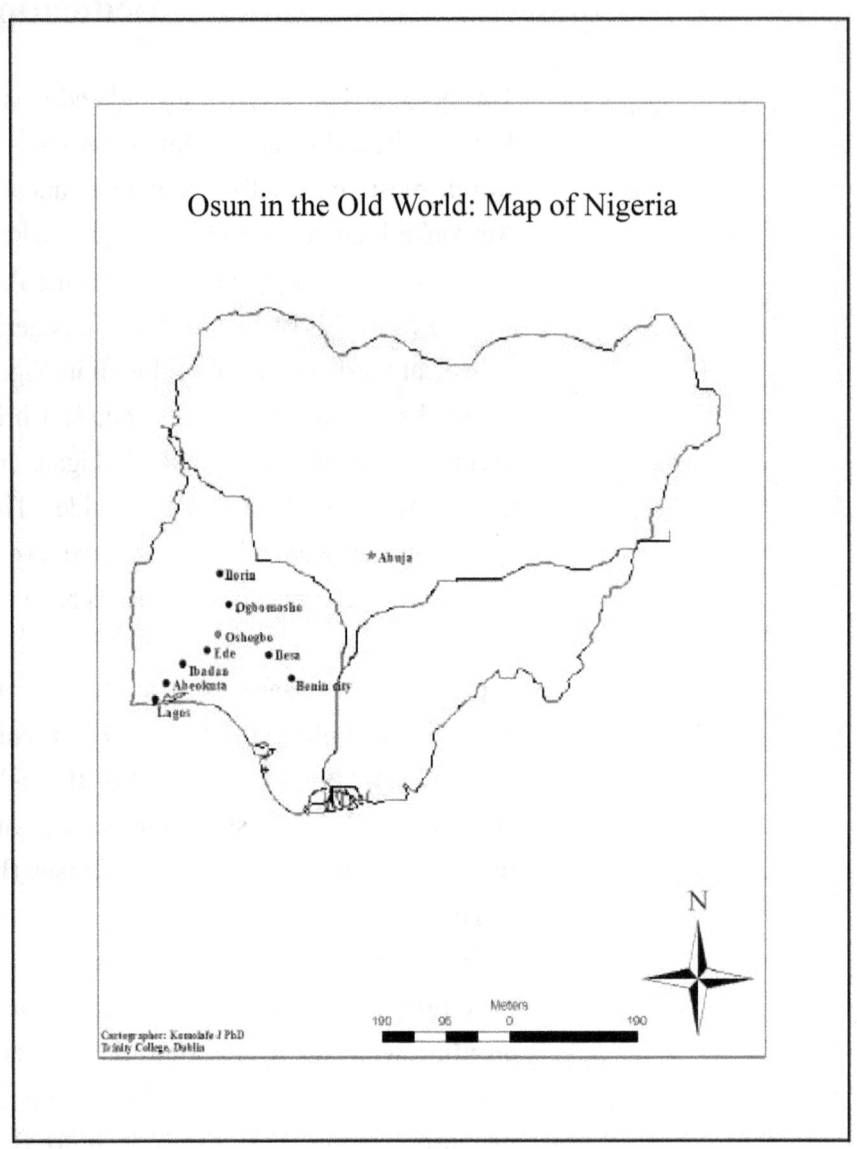

Copyright Dr. Julius Komolafe, Geography, Trinity College, Dublin Ireland 2008

Foreward

Adewale Kuyebi, Ph.D., a learned scholar in religion, is also a gifted storyteller. Of African descent, he has impressively merged his African experiences with Western learning and produced an absorbing portrait of Osun, the notable female Yoruba deity who originated in Osogbo, Nigeria, and eventually won adherents in both North and South America.

Over many centuries and in different countries Osun has been variously known and revered also as Osum, Oshun, Ochun, Oxum or Oxun. Previous publications have generally concentrated on Osun in Africa or on her new life in the Americas. Dr. Kuyebi has successfully described Osun's life on both sides of the Atlantic. The account is colourful and fascinating on several levels, with special attention to myth as a form of oral history and religious poetry.

The annual highlight of Osun's worship continue to be her festival, celebrated in Osogbo, Nigeria. Colourful and dynamic the festival celebrates and also interprets to Osun's followers the significance of such symbols as water, colours, numbers, dance, music, ritual, sacred places and names as well as the importance of certain animals. These and other sustaining elements have kept Osun's memory alive in people's minds on the African and American continents.

Despite a measure of intolerance outside its native country, in the learned judgment of Dr. Kuyebi, Osun's worship has survived and grown due to Osun's indigenous power to rekindle the memories of the past as well as to integrate African culture in different societies.

Throughout this fascinating book, Dr. Kuyebi has been remarkably successful in keeping alive the reader's continued interest. The powerful myth of Osun is alive today.

                                    Egil Grislis,
                                    Department of Religion,
                                    Professor emeritus,
                                    St.John's College,
                                    The University of Manitoba,
                                    Winnipeg, Manitoba, Canada

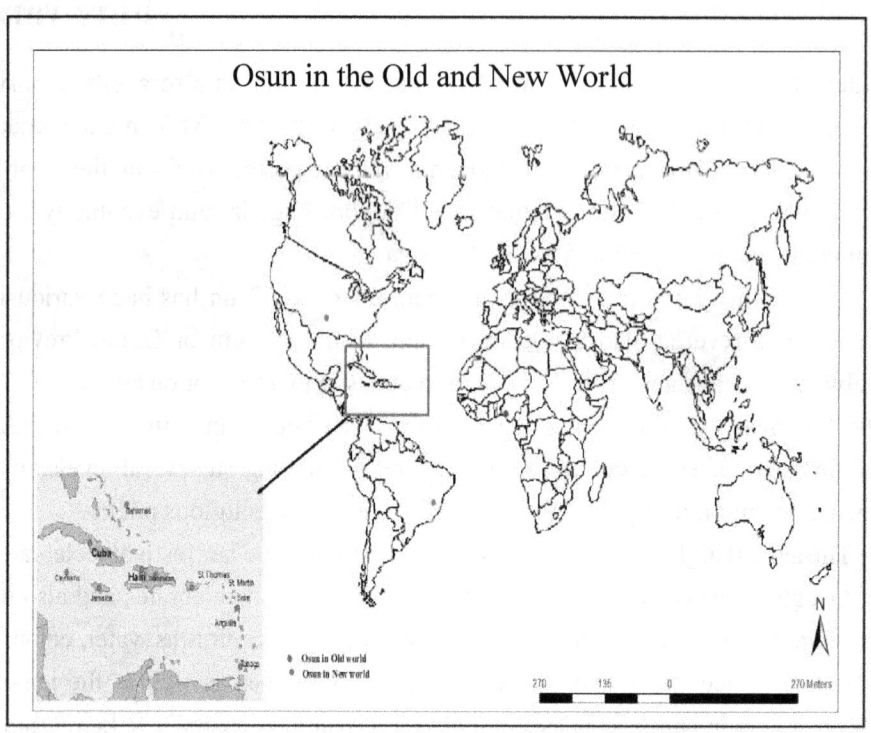

Copyright Dr. Julius Komolafe, Geography, Trinity College, Dublin Ireland 2008

Introduction

This book examines Osun worship in the Old and the New World, and argues that the Yoruba myths contribute to the continuation of Osun worship and veneration in Africa and the Americas today. The first part of this book is devoted to the treatment of religious methodologies in Yoruba studies in the New and the Old Worlds. Its second part explains that myths sustain the Osun festival in Osogbo, Yorubaland. It establishes the fact that Osun myths dominate the history of Osogbo and its rulership. The third part of this book deals with the impacts of Osun myths in the New World religion. The Old World is the Yorubaland, and the New World are the continents of North America, South America, and West Indies; all are in the western hemisphere. The New World is also referred to as the Americas in the religious studies. We argue for the continuity of Osun myths and establish the importance of Yoruba tradition in the Americas as a phenomenon that cannot be ignored by any serious student of religion. It also supports the argument that the Yoruba slaves brought Osun worship to the New World and they merged some of its aspects into Santeria.

Contents

1. African Traditional Religion   1
   Methods Applied in Studying African Traditional Religion
   in the New World   4
   Myths in Yoruba Religious Study   8
   Previous Methodologies Applied in Studying Osun
   in Yorubaland   14

2. Osun Osogbo   18
   Osun, the daughter of Olodumare   18
   Olodumare, "God" in Yoruba Belief   18
   Meanings and spellings of Osun   20
   Osogbo: Osun's Original Setting   33

3. Celebrating Osun in Osogbo   59
   Atupa Olojumeridinlogun "the Sixteen-Face Lamps"   61
   The Day of the Festival   65
   Major Participants in the Annual Festival   70
   Other Important Places and Things Associated
   with the Osun   80
   Summary of the Osun Festival   93

4 Osun in the New World   96
   How did the Yoruba get to the New World?   99
   Osun in the New World   100

5. Osun in Cuba   104
   The Africans as Lucumi   107

Contents

African Religion in Cuba	110
Yoruba Religion in Cuba	110
Osun Worship in Cuba	111
Osun in Santeria	117
6. Osun in Brazil	**129**
African Myths in Brazil	130
The Yoruba in Brazil as Nago Community	132
Challenges Encountered by Yoruba Worshippers in Brazil	136
The Yoruba Religion in Catholic Faith	138
7. Osun in Trinidad, Jamaica and in Haiti	**148**
Osun in Trinidad	148
Osun in Jamaica	158
Osun in Haiti	160
8. Osun Worship and Mythological Studies	**170**
9. Mythological Studies in the History of Religion	**189**
Ferdinard de Saussure (1857-1913)	189
Claude Levi Strauss (1908-2009)	190
Carl G. Jung (1875-1961)	193
Mircea Eliade (1907-1986)	195
Rudolf Bultmann (1884-1976)	197
Conclusion	198
Bibliography	201

Osun in the New World: Map of Brazil

Osun in the New World: Map of Cuba

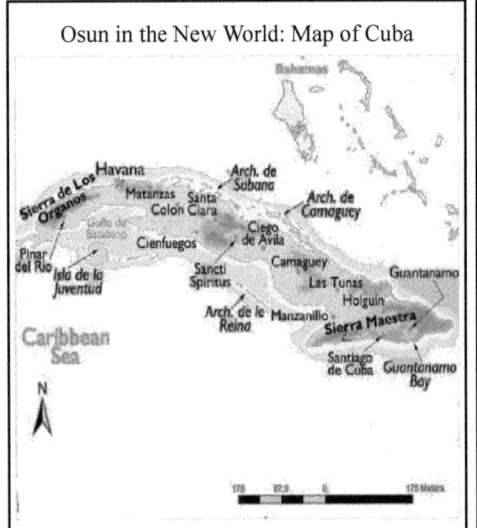

Osun in the New World: Map of Jamaica

1

African Traditional Religion

Our aim is to describe the phenomena effects of myths in the *orisha* (divinities) worship or veneration in the Old World and the New World. But before we do that, we want to review some selected methodologies that have been applied to the study of African religion in the New World and the Old World in order to justify our use of the continuation of the mythological method in this study.

Most of the States and Federal government-owned universities in Nigeria have faculties of African Religion; and their most favoured method of teaching religion is called Comparative Religion. By adopting such a narrowly focused method, many religious students are only able to research into different African religious sects and religious activities. Nigerian African religious students are paying less attention to the interdisciplinary study of religion and politics which was the focused methodology before this time. As a testimonial to this, Benjamin Ray states that "the study of African religions has recently emerged from the shadow of African politics, history and sociology and has become something of a specialised field with a sizeable body of literature" (Okpewho and Mazuri: xix).

African religious study is popularly known as African Traditional Religion; its popular acronomy is ATR. African Traditional Religion is, by nature, an oral religion, there are not many well-equipped libraries in Nigeria to do much work on non-African religious studies (Cox 1992: 35-37). Religions of eastern and central Asia share many religious aspects with the Yoruba religion, but they have more writing materials in libraries than the African religious sects. Sacrifice, rituals, music, dance, poetry, prose and spirit-possession are common practices where religious students get new information for their researches (Omofolabo 1998: 1).

African traditional religion, in general, is understood to be community-based and faith-inclusive. It encourages people to support each other during their different religious group meetings and festivals. Its religious symbols and objects are available for students to study (Warner-Lewis 1999: 22). African descendants in other parts of the world still honor, observe and worship the African divinities according to the received knowledge of their ancestors (Platvoet, Cox and Olupona 1996: 23). This also is available for us all to be examined.

Some scholars misinterpret African religion by calling it many derogatory names which often give it a low opinion in religious studies. Due to lack of understanding of the religion, some scholars use such terms as 'primitive' and 'barbaric' to describe African religion. This is probably due to the practice of some inhuman and savage acts during rituals and sacrifices to both animals and fellow human-beings (Cannon 1942: 169). In *Ogun* sacrifice, for example, priests practise the cutting off of dogs' heads with sharp knives and sprinkle their blood on the altars in public. Also, *oro* worshippers are still expected to observe a daylight or daytime curfew during the festival. *Oro* festival is thought to be too secretive for male-novices, children and women to be part of it in Yorubaland. African religious activities are not opened to all people, and if anybody proves stubborn, such people may lose their lives through spiritual and physical attacks. Such practices intend to protect the integrity of the community beliefs and to protect the community from evil and morally reprehensible behaviours. For them, African religious festivals are a celebration of mythological figures that have historical, religious, political or social importance to a family or a community (Vansina 1985, 2006). Kings, chiefs, priests and priestesses are part of the festivals.

One well-known anthropologist who studied Yoruba religion and culture is Geoffrey Parrinder. He spent twenty-four years writing on the characteristics of the West African religion and its people, including the Yorubas (Platvoet 1992, 1996: 113; Parrinder 1951, 1976). Parrinder focuses on documenting the characteristics of the West African traditional religion. Michael F. C. Bourdillon also studies what the different religious groups had in common in Africa (Bourdillon 1996: 145). He helps us to understand the West African world view through their religious practices.

Scholars who write about the African traditional religions without being initiated into them are often considered "outsiders" and their works superficial. Such scholars are often thought by worshippers to be ignorant. However, non-initiated religious scholars, who did not succumb to the community pressure, have freedom to write and interpret their religious findings in any way suitable to their conscience. They have no fear of exposing any discrepancies in the teachings and practices of any religious groups. However, in those days, one of the ways to get an authentic knowledge of the African religion is to become a member. Scholars who had been initiated into a particular African religion are usually thought to have a better knowledge of the religion but perform poorly in making the information public (Mason 2002: 3). Keeping some sensitive information confidential is a form of allegiance of such people. This kind of blind-obedience is mandatory in most of the African religious practices for the following reason.

> Within the religion itself, secrecy also protects ritual knowledge and the power it implies. The ethos of secrecy plays an important role in the religion of the *orichas* among the Yoruba, as many ritual practices are secret and only accessible to initiated priestesses and priests (Mason 2002: 9).

To have access to detailed knowledge of a religion "one must be initiated to privy to those actions; second, if one is privy by rites of initiation, then one is equally constrained by that responsibility" not to divulge the secrecy to the non-members (Badejo 1996: 135). Certainly, it is too bad that the knowledge of secret practices could not be freely shared in academic meetings. Let it be known that the knowledge that is not shared would remain untested.

After joining a cult, if one later discloses unauthorized materials to the public, such a person may not receive another opportunity to visit the shrine again and may never gain the audience of the worshippers. Even worse, religious fanatics may, in defence of their faith, launch spiritual or physical attacks on the author. Parrinder, Wenger and those who voluntarily join the African religious cults, usually describe the observable facts of religious practices with such caution without being critical in their presentation.

Scholars, who did not want to be initiated into any particular religion before they could research their topics on the field, had to rely on second-hand resourceful people (Ray 2000: xiii). Such information could be verified by contacting *babalawo* "herbalists" who share the myths of religions with scholars who are willing to pay consultation fees (Parrinder 1962: 100-101).

Methods Applied in Studying African Religion in the New World
In view of all the circumstances and conditions surrounding the study of Yoruba religion, we observed that the majority of the western scholars who study the African traditional religion become its members, or at least, were very sympathetic to the indigenous faith. It is understandable that a few of them became converts in order to win the trust of the natives and to learn more about the peoples' religion by participating in their rituals. At one point in time, Mason explained his experience as a member of the African religion in the New World.

> I have used a generalized description for two reasons: First: as mentioned, each *asiento* has its variations and special preparations, which do not bear on my basic point about human social activity's creating and maintaining the social presence of the *orichas*. Second, Santeria elders do not want to make too much information available to the public and it would be impossible for an unauthorized person to use this generalized account to generate the ritual (Mason 2002: 61).

By describing the preparation of rituals and sacrifices, he attempts to play it safe in order not to anger the devotees. Scholars who had been initiated into a particular religion are sensitive to the priests and devotees' feelings in the sharing of their knowledge in public. The scholars who are not interested in African spirituality in the New World often choose to study the subject of African religion and politics, education, slavery, social intergration and economics.

Eugino Matibag studies the Afro-Cuban religion by using myths (Matibag 1996: 4). For people who took a similar approach, religious stories and slaves' experiences are rich sources for reconstructing African beliefs in the New World. Such stories contain related subjects on political, economic, social and cultural improvements (Warner-Lewis 1999: 22). However, religious scholars were too much consumed with slavery themes rather than religious issues in the African-American historiography of the 1970s and 1980s (Inikori 1999: 49).

The initial efforts of those focused on the effects of African religion in the New World led to the use of the term "syncretism". Syncretism is an academic term that students of religion use loosely to describe what happens to the African religion when it comes in contact with other religions in the Americas (Evans: 379-380). In other words, syncretism is an appropriate descriptive term for explaining how the African traditional religion blends with one or more other world religions.

Specifically, syncretism is a process whereby African religious elements are mixed with Christianity in the New World. Syncretism is a religious phenomenon of adaptation and accommodation of the new religious groups by the mainline religious groups.

Herskovits, in his research of eclectic and multicultural Afro-American religions, sponsors the term 'syncretism' as a religious phenomenon in the New World (Houk 1986, 1992). His works are a collection of diverse voices and discourses, and since then, syncretism has become a religious term in describing the merging of two or more religions. For Matibag "a syncretic artifact is not a synthesis, but a signifier made out of difference" (Matibag 1996: 11). This thought and term was supported by Melville J. Herskovits and Roger Bastide. They all emphasized the accommodative, acculturative and syncretive natures of African religions in Western countries (Glazier 1996: 420-421). In effect African religion eventually gave birth to Santeria and voodoo. Where new religions did not emerge, the West African religions had transformed the western-oriented religions, most especially Cuban Catholicism (Matibag 1996: 1). African religion, the Yoruba religion in particular, had been adopted in the New World as their home (Matibag 1996: 52-53).

The terms accommodation, and acculturation are other terms which are used in describing the encounters of the African religion with the American religion. Negatively or positively, the effects of adaptability of religious elements in the New World cannot be denied by religious scholars. In doing this, Bascom made a clear distinction between fact and fiction of myths of the Yoruba religion in the New World (Okpewho 1980: 7-9).

Another popular method that scholars have used in understanding the history of African religion in the New World is called the "reinterpretation method." *Reinterpretation* is a method whereby scholars read cultural traits of oral religion as typology of the scriptural religions (Evans: 380). The official doctrines of new religions, especially Catholicism and Islam, are considered more reliable than the traditional religions of the Old World (Evans: 379-380). Ironically, the Euro-Americans are more fascinated by the African traditional religious expressions than the Black-Americans. Here is a testimony to that effect, "finally it is interesting to note a further process of acculturation: the adoption of many of these instruments by Americans of non-African ancestry" (Evans: 386). Religious ecstasy, dancing, drumming and conjuring of spirits are attracting non-African people to the African religion.

A few other scholars who address the Afro-Cuban religious elements and reinterpretation of it in the New World are: Fernando Ortiz, Romulo Lachatanere, Alejo Carpenter, Jose Antonio Ramos, Lydia Cabrera, Nicolas Guillen, Nancy Morejon, Miguel Barnet, Guillermo Cabrera Infante, Antonio Benitez Rojo and Manuel Cofino (Matibag 1996: 4). Due to the multitudes of African languages and different levels of meanings in their practices, some scholars found it challenging to interpret African religious elements involved in the Americas. One must have a skill in linguistic analyses in working with African related religion. It is easier to see the impact of African religion on American culture and religion, but it would be a very challenging work to determine its linguistic origin, and to determine where such influences originated from in Africa (Bascom 1969; Oruka 1983: 388). There is an urgent need to account for the importance of Yoruba myths in the Americas, most especially Osun myths in the New World (Bascom 1969). For many African-Americans are beginning to view Osun as an American figure, which is far from the truth.

Writing about the African traditional religion's encounters with the New World religious practices will be too broad a scope to cover in a book of this size. It is, therefore, reasonable to focus on a particular divinity such as Osun. This is not a totally new academic adventure in religious studies. A very helpful book on Osun came out very recently, which was edited by Joseph M. Murphy and Mei-Mei Sanford, titled *Osun Across the Waters: A Yoruba Goddess in Africa and the Americas* (Murphy and Sanford 2001: 1). This book is a collection of essays on Osun and other related subjects. The intention of the authors is to find the historical and cultural significance of Yoruba traditions in the Americas (Murphy and Sanford 2001: 1). Seventeen scholars write on different aspects of Osun in the New World. Unfortunately, the book offers its readers little information on Osun worship in Osogbo. Also, each contributor uses different methodology and focuses on different aspects of Osun in isolation of the others' essays (Castellanons 2001: 34-45; Murphy 2001: 87-101). No storyline was provided to really apprectiate their collective works.

In the book mentioned above, little attention was paid to the chronological developments of Osun myths. As the contributors touched various aspects of the Osun story their essays significantly established the importance of Osun, but each essay is disjointed from the other (Murphy and Sanford 2001:1). References are made to the influence of Osun in different parts of Yoruba cities such as Ikoro Ekiti and Ijumu in Kwara State, but none of the contributors examine the Osun festival in Osogbo or anywhere in the world.

Myths in Yoruba Religious Studies

Instead of using African traditional religion or looking for the reinterpretation of African traditional religion, we are using the descriptive structuralism approach to study the significance of myth in studying an *orisa*, Osun, in both sides of the Atlantic. It is an anthropological method that is associated with Claude Levi-Strauss that seeks to analyze social relationships in terms of abstract relational structure which are often expressed in a logical symbolism such as color, dressing, figures, numbers, rocks, forests, rivers, and so on. It is a method of analysing how language is spoken by a group of people in an oral community. It is a study that describes the interrelation of each religious practice as they relate to the organized whole within a religious community.

Currently, critical theories such as structural approach have become useful in studying religion in higher education levels, especially at the university level. It helps in grasping the obscure concepts of people's everyday experience. By applying a particular critical theory, one learns to see other cultures and religion in meaningful ways. Critical theory is helpful in thinking logically, creatively, and to have a better insight into the practices of other peoples' cultures. As well, it provides a better way to raise questions on the devotees' assumptions and values of religions without passing judgement on them.

Toyin Falola and Ann Genova argue for the use of myth in determining the structural elements in a religion by saying that "creativity among the Yoruba has a long history. The traditions of oral histories, story telling, performance and dramas, all became part of their habits of civilization, and have continued to this day" (Falola and Genova 2005: 1). Therefore, African religious scholars have used oral sources to explain the Yoruba people's religion and belief. They have studied African oral literature to determine how influential the African people are around the world (Okpewho, Boyce Davis, and Mazrui: 275; Owomoyela 1971: 275). Bascom reminds us of the significance of Yoruba oral literature as a conceptual framework in reconstructing the general history of the Africans in the world. He argues that it is possible to reconstruct African history out of their oral narratives (Bascom 1981: 67). From one year to another, one can see the similarities in the story telling, performance and dramas of their festivals (Olajubu 1970; Olatunji 69-86). Irving Hexham argues such stories could become myths depending on "the use to which the content is put" (Hexham 1981: 31).

In the Yoruba festival, one can find historical, cultural and social elements merging together to form religious structures in their religious symbols. In daily practices, there are useful repetitive comparisons in Yoruba riddles, etiquette, play, drama and religious festivals that hold the community together (Adedeji 1971: 135). The Yoruba community observes such customs to reinforce the honor of their divinities (Owomoyela 1971: 123). The Yoruba religious festivals are rooted in the daily common cultural and religious mythological beliefs (Mbon 1996: 175-176; Vansina 2006). There are many lessons to be learned in Yoruba religions and culture if one is meticulous enough to compare and contrast the contents of surviving myths (Mbon 1996: 178).

No matter what kind of methodological approach one uses in the study of Yoruba religion, everybody has to work with myths. In religious studies, for instance, Hackett calls for "the descriptive phenomenology" approach to the study of Yoruba religion (Mbon 1996: 178; Hackett 1988: 43). Others have argued for a more critical analysis and comparison of religious activities. As we compare the contents of the survived myths, we will be able to see the cross-cultural and cross-continental value of the Yoruba oral literature in today's religious developments (Deidre 1995: xiv). As of today, the Yoruba religion has grown beyond its cultural and geographical boundaries, which are the West African countries. We are of the opinion that if we can compare the religious elements of myths that survive in Yorubaland with those in the New World, we will come to the conclusion that the Osun of the New World is essentially the same Osun of Osogbo.

In its most literal sense, myth usually means false beliefs. To say something is a myth implies it is non-existent. But this general idea of myth may be misleading in religious studies; therefore, it is essential to consider different theories of myth. This is a selective rather than an exhaustive treatment of the various theories of myth. These lists demonstrate a variety of theories that could be used to establish the significance of descriptive myth in oral literature. Under critical reviews, myth has been classified into evolutionism, psychoanalysis, diffusionism, functionalism, symbolism, formalism and structuralism (Okpewho, vii). Some theorists see myth as "the perspective of *individual* units of ideas" which are below the standard of what the evolutionists, the psychoanalysts and the biologists would endorse (Okpewho: 20).

Diffusionism defines the origin of myths as the result of "historical contact and geographical contiguity between people" (Okpewho: 15). People who adopted this perspective include: William Bascom, Alan Dundes, Stith Thompson, Elias Lonnrot, Richard M. Dorson, Antti Aarne, May A. Klipple, Roger Abrahams, Kenneth W. Clarke and Arewa Ojo (Okpewho: 17-18). The diffusionism perspective requires that one pay adequate attention to similarities in myths. As myths move from one cultural context to another, different aspects of myths' details are emphasized more in a new local context than in its original context. Whenever myths are studied, scholars have to pay attention to all available versions and variants of each myth in order to reconstruct it.

Functionalism is the second generation of oral narrative theorists which sees "human culture in terms of related *forms* as an aid to the understanding either of social organization, or of cultural thought, or else of creative activity: this generation is represented, respectively, by functionalists, symbolists, and formalists" (Okpewho: 20). It is a late nineteenth century American school of psychology approach. They wanted to determine how the mind functions to adapt the individual to the environment. The method stresses the interdependence of the patterns in a society and their efforts in maintaining religious, cultural and social unity. Bronislaw Kasper Malinowski (1884-1942), an anthropologist, represents the functionalist branch of mythologists. This group of scholars taught that myths are the functional unity of the society and one of the reasons people achieve harmonious living and social stability. Without myths, conflicts and chaos would prevail in the community against justice and equity. Hence, social activities and cultural facts are preserved in myths. Myths function as a way to provide rule of succession and sustainability of community instructions, institutions, and structure.

Functionalism understands myths to be the tales of society. To them, myths answer the questions of origin of the people. As narrative stories, myths vary from content to content; we heard that "there are many stories in Black Africa concerned with the origins of the people – not just creation stories and other mythical narratives of the way things were 'in the beginning,' but stories concerned with historical progenitors and their heroic accomplishments" (Abrahams: 231). These sorts of myths explain and validate various beliefs and ritual practices among the people. They "act as 'charters' of present social institutions rather than as faithful *historical* records of times past" (Okpewho: 24). Such myths therefore create and sustain a sense of "togetherness, homogeneity and cohesion" (Okpewho: 24).

Functionalism interprets myths as symbols. This interpretation goes back to the eighteenth century theories of C. G. Heyne, Friedrich Crueuzer, and J. J. Bachofen (Okpewho: 26-27). Sigmund Freud (1856-1939), an Austrian neurologist, and Carl Gustav Jung (1875-1961), a Swiss psychologist, adopted this mythological theory in their works. C. S. Pierce and W. Marshall Urban further analyzed the structure of symbolic activity (Okpewho: 27). Myths are an advance on the development of language; language motivated the creativity of mythmaking. Our theoretical approach will therefore make use of linguistic, contextual, and historical analyses. Myths reflect and explain social, religious, and economic realities of a community. It is therefore one's task to understand the images and symbols of the tales. One has to explain the symbols in ritual, for each of them have meanings in their cultural contexts (Okpewho: 29). Water, blood, words, color and other symbols have meanings in the context of myths. During sacrifices, the rate of the emission of blood from the sacrificial animals is symbolic. Even, the red color of sap from the plants conveniently links the community to a logical, intellectual appreciation of Yoruba myths. Sap is essential to life, health, and vigor in Yoruba thought.

Another school that propones a theory of oral narrative is that of formalism. This theory pays attention to arrangement, style, and artistic form of literature but deemphasizes its literary contents. For them, myths function as ways of preserving the practice of the prescribed community norms. Myths are thought to be in categories, with corresponding deemphasising the contents but exaggerating the messages behind the stories. We have animal tales, tales proper, and anecdotes (jokes) (Okpewho: 31). The anecdotes or ancedota are unpublished stories, but popular short stories in the community. Such narratives are very interesting, amusing, and contain biographical incident which may not necessarily be factual. In short, myths are abstractions of the society; one has to study the patterns and techniques. They have artistic liberties in conveying the attitudes and emotions through nontraditional and unrepresentational means.

All of the theories of myths mentioned above support the fact that there are useful materials in myths in understanding people, culture and context.

We can therefore compare and contrast forms and themes of myths, cultures and contexts of myths, peoples and places of myths in academic works. Myths have cultural symbolic meanings. They are dynamic and transportable to other contexts and able to transform people, places and cultures.

There are still other various theories that can be used to study the nature and function of myth in religious studies, but because this is not our main focus, we just need to list them. Some of these critical theories are: Psychoanalytical Criticism, Marxist Criticsm, Feminist Criticism, Structuralist Criticism, Deconstructive Criticism, African American Criticism, Postcolonial Criticism and so on. But the most relevant theoretical approach for the study of myth is structuralism. For a fuller understanding of myth in Yoruba religion in the Old and the New Worlds, it is necessary to briefly examine the theories of myth by Claude Levi-Strauss (1908-) a Belgium born social anthropologist, Ferdinand de Saussure (1857-1913), Carl G. Jung (1875-1961), Mircea Eliade (1907-1986), and Rudolf Karl Bultmann (1884-1976), a German theologian. However, we still suspend our discussion or reflection on Structuralism to the latter part of this book. As you read along, hold on to your thoughts because we are applying a descriptive structural methodology in this book. Our observation and experience in reading will be factually grounded in informative rather than based on normative, prescriptive, or emotive cultural studies.

Previous Methodologies Applied in Studying Osun in Yorubaland
This is a book that deals with the structure of Yoruba language with less emphasis on the comparative elements with other major world religions. Looking back to the methods that early researchers used in the study of Yoruba religion, we noticed that most limited the scope of their study to Yoruba kingdoms. They usually focus on subjects that are geographically

limited to Yoruba people in Yorubaland. Such works presumed that Yorubaland is a homogenous community, having the same uniform structure and composition throughout a cultural neighborhood. There is a need to remind the students of religions that the Yoruba religion had spread beyond Yorubaland. This is one of the reasons why we aim at examining the common religious practices in Osun worship in the Old and the New Worlds to advance the argument that the Yoruba religion in an international one.

Various scholars have written books and articles on aspects of Osun in an attempt to document her effect on the lives of her worshippers outside Nigeria. One such book is *"Osun Seegesi: the Elegant Deity of Wealth"* written by Deidre L. Badejo. The author focuses on Osun's personality and the rituals in Osun festivals (Ray 2000: 78). Her conclusion was that the Osun festival is an annual religious carnival. In her understanding, the "Osun Festival and its oral literature provide the context, content, meaning, and symbolism that mirror the complexities of sacred and secular dramatic art" (Badejo 1996: 135). This is not a total interpretation of Osun. We would argue that these symbols, actions and architectural decorations have spiritual significance and meaning to the worshippers (Ojo 1979: 335). Sacred traditions have been retained and sustained in different forms of ideas, attitudes, sentiments and the people's thoughts, and this has formed the basis of their belief (Adedeji 1971: 135). It is a major challenge to recall the whole story without the annual religious festival (Bascom 1967: 52).

Badejo also thought of the Osun festival as an annually staged event. The drumming, singing and the number of the crowds that paraded on the streets of Osogbo during the festival misled her (Badejo 1996: 135). The correct interpretation of what people do and see during religious festival matters in documentation (Beier 1977: 13).

Another thing we observed in Badejo's work was her socio-cultural approach to the study of the Osun festival (Badejo 1996: 168). Badejo rightly described Yoruba culture and religion as deeply rooted in hierarchical and patriarchal settings. Osun stands out in balancing gender equality among the Yoruba divinities and Yoruba people. Both men and women respect Osun's personhood and divinity in Yorubaland.

Drama is a mere act of impersonation, a play, theatrical performance, and dramatic art for the purpose of entertainment. Osun is not a drama for it will not be an adequate element in reconstructing the essence of a religious festival. Most Yoruba festivals are not fairy tales or mere memorial holidays. Most of the activities involved are religiously and spiritually significant to the community (Osogbo Cultural Heritage Council, *Osun Osogbo Festival*: 3).

We take issue with the title of the book, *Osun Seegesi: the Elegant Deity of Wealth, Power, and Femininity* (Deidre 1995). The author claims that Osun is the deity of wealth, power and feminity. The attributes mentioned are not popularly known as Osun's in Yoruba thought. It is debatable that Osun gave up her wealth in order to bear a child. This interpretation may be based on *Odu Ifa* "oral oracle" but generally, Osun has little connection with economic development in Yoruba history (Bascom 1943: 127).

As mentioned earlier, we have some scholars who had studied Osun in the Old World but with strictly biased and prejudiced mindsets. They have a fixed mental attitude and inclination to side with the religious people. One example of those who embraced a Yoruba deity was Sussan Wenger who came from Austria. She converted to Osun worship and made the Osun shrine her home for over thirty years. She was so loyal to Osun that she became one of her female officials. The Osogbo leadership accepted her commitment and gave Sussan Wenger a local chieftaincy title known as Adunni Olorisa (Beier 1977: 11). *Adunni* means "precious to have" and *olorisa* means "an idol worshipper," a reference to her devotion to Osun. Osun became Sussan Wenger's metaphysical mother figure (Beier 1977: 20). She also understood Osun to be a metaphysical mother of Osogbo people (Beier 1977: 20).

Another example of participant-researchers, which is another name for the positivist anthropologists, was Mason. He went through a series of initiations during the time of his research (Mason 2002: 3). Mason was initiated into the Osun worship because he wanted to have inside knowledge of the religion in Cuba (Farrow 1996: 14). His involvements with the worship reflected in his conclusion when he wrote:

> This description reflects these generalized accounts as well as fifteen initiations in which I have participated in Cuba and the United States. It reflects the commonalities of initiations for the most common *orichas*: Chango, Obatala, Ochun, and Yemaya (Mason 2002: 61).

His interpretation became suspicious because he became the promoter of the religion instead of doing a critical analysis of it. Let us hear the stories of the personhood of Osun.

2
Osun Osogbo

Just a reminder, the question we are concerned about in this book is to determine whether Osun in the New World is the same as the Osun of the Old World. In answering the question, we need to study the selected myths and the recurring religious elements of Osun worship in Osogbo. Osun and Osogbo are historically and geographically inseparable (Olupona 2001: 49). Then, who is Osun, and where is Osogbo? Let us discuss the subject in brief.

A. Osun, the Daughter of *Olodumare*

Before we narrate the Osun festival, first of all, we must examine the personhood of Osun among other Yoruba divinities. The significance of this section is to support the Yoruba belief that there is cosmological order and unity in the Yoruba worldview. This orderliness is obvious in creation, divinities, human beings, death and the afterlife. It exists in this order: God, gods/goddesses, ancestors, kings, men, women, and children (Omoyajowo 1975).

B. *Olodumare* "God" in Yoruba Belief

In Yoruba thought, God is known as *Olodumare*. Olodumare is the lord over all Yoruba divinities and human beings because he created the divinities and all other living beings (Greene 1996: 115ff). The Yoruba believe in one supreme God, *Olorun Olodumare*. Yoruba people honor *Olodumare* and recognize *Oduduwa* as the arch-ancestor of the Yoruba (Abimbola 1994: 75-76). Wande Abimbola summarized the attributes of Olodumare.

> ...*Olodumare*, the Yoruba High God has no cult of his own among the humans. He also has no temples or shrines. Sacrifices are never made to him. Consequently, Olodumare has no liturgy, iconography, or priesthood. He is the supreme example of an abstract divinity too mighty to be captured by any artistic, literary, or idealistic simplification (Abimbola 1994: 76-77).

Olodumare exists in the thoughts and minds of every Yoruba. Olodumare has a lot of similarities with the God of other religions. Sandra Greene has argued that African thoughts and practices of a supreme being change from time to time and from one tribe to another (Greene 1996: 115ff).

Unlike divinities, Olodumare does not have a day or month set apart to worship him. All ordinary divinities have special days of worship and festival. But in Yoruba thought, every time people honor divinities, they are indirectly contacting Olodumare. He deals directly with human beings.

Osun is one divinity through whom the Yoruba relate to God. The other members of *Orisa (*divinities) are *egungun* masquerades*, oro, Obatala/Orisa-nla, Orunmila/ Ifa, Sango, Oya, Iyemoja, Osun Osogbo, Esulalu, Orisa oko, Sonpona, orisa ibeji and Osanyin.* All divinities owe their existence and personhood to Olodumare (Idowu 1973: 159). They are emissaries of *Olodumare,* God in Yoruba belief. From the beginning, all divinities originated from heavens where God resides. Olodumare is the father and mother of the divinities. All divinities function and serve as Olodumare's emissaries. Each divinity has special priests, temples, religious communities and seasons of worship. In religious festivals, such as the Osun festival, the religious elements mentioned are means of informing, educating and promoting the belief of divinity in the communities. Divinities, nature and social institutions are embodied in God. But, the Yoruba God cannot be represented in any form or image.

C. Meanings and Spellings of Osun

In our earlier discussions, we addressed the meanings of Osun as a Yoruba word, which had various spelling variances in the New World. The question then is: what is the right spelling? "Osun" is a Yoruba word. It is a name of a female divinity that is closely tied to Osogbo. Her name is spelled in different ways because of the 's' sound that is 'ch' in Yoruba pronunciation. It could be spelled Osun with a dot under the 's' as in Yoruba language spelling, or in any of the following forms: Oshun, Ochun, or Oxun (Badejo 1996: 53). They are refer to the same goddess from Yorubaland.

The word "Osun" means "to seep out" or "a source" from which something seeps out. It is from the word *orisun,* meaning "the primary source" in the Yoruba language (Deidre 1995: 53). We need to note here that Yoruba word-study is an interesting area of linguistic analysis of words, sentences, or proverbs and grammar (Bamgbose 1968: 79).

Spelling variations are of less significance, because the same Osun is later known and honored in other West African countries. The river Osun is a physical representation of Osun in Yorubaland. Ifa oracles and the practice of divination aided people in different parts of the world in remembering Osun. Ifa divination "is practiced not only by the Yoruba, but by the inhabitants of Dahomey and Togoland as well, and in the New World by the Negroes of Brazil and Cuba" (Bascom 1943: 130). Wherever you find Ifa, you find Osun.

As we have indicated previously, Osun is the only female divinity of the seventeen Yoruba divinities (Badejo 1996: 58). Oduduwa is the arch-divinity. He acts like the earthly father for all of them. Here is an interesting Yoruba myth that shows how Osun gave birth to children:

> Yemaja. – Before Obatala was deserted by Odudua, she is said to have borne him a son and daughter, Aganju and Yemaja respectively. This brother and sister eventually married and had a son Orungan, who

committed incest with his mother, Yemaja. She fled from him in horror and shame, but he pursued her until she fell. Her body swelled to a great size; from her breasts flowed streams of water which became a lagoon, and from her body issued a number of different orishas, including Shango (the god of lightning), Oya (the Niger), Oshun, Oba (three rivers which became the three wives of Shango), Olokun (god of the sea), Olosa (the lagoon-goddess), Orishako (farm-god) (Farrow 1996: 46).

This is not a popular myth in Yorubaland, but that does not mean it does not exist in certain parts of the Yoruba kingdom.

Osun, as a special divinity of Osogbo, rules and protects the people from dangers and wars. Unlike most other divinities, Osun is not a seasonal goddess. She is active all year round. On the contrary, Sango the god of thunder and lightning is active only during the rainy season. A Yoruba proverb says, *enikan ki bu Sango leru,* meaning no one invokes Sango during the dry season (Bamgbose 1968: 80-86). He would not respond or act on behalf of the devotee during the dry season.

1. Osun, the Ruler of Osogbo: Osun rules Osogbo in conjunction with the kings. Oba Gbadewolu Larooye was the first *Atewogbeja* of Osogbo (Osogbo Cultural Heritage Council 1994: 14). Owa Laege was Larooye's father. Laege was originally from Ilesa, a Yoruba city near Osogbo. Larooye's mother was Tekulu, one of the princesses of Alaafin of the old Oyo Empire, another Yoruba group in Yorubaland. Osun is a hospitable divinity. She honors people of different dialects and works well with the living and the living-dead, otherwise known as ancestors. With the help of Osun, Larooye reigned over the Osogbo people between 1670 and 1760 (Osogbo Cultural Heritage Council, *Osun Osogbo Festival*: 3). Larooye's first palace at Osogbo was built on the spot where the Ile Osun, Osun temple, is situated today (Osogbo Cultural Heritage Council, *Osun Osogbo Festival*: 9). The first palace was built on the Osun floods canal (Osogbo Cultural Heritage Council, *Osun Osogbo Festival*: 18). When there was a flood, the first settlers had to move to a higher ground.

According to historical Yoruba beliefs, kings are semi-gods in nature and in authority. It adds more dignity to the personhood of Osun as all the people in Osogbo, including the kings, recognize the authority of Osun. The official title of the king is "Ataoja" which means one who spreads his hands to welcome the fish of the Osun River during the Osun festival. Osun's authority is widely recognized among the Yoruba (Beier 1977: 18). All prospective kings of Osogbo, otherwise known as the Ataoja of Osogbo were religiously, physically and psychologically prepared by oral tradition for the throne of Osogbo. The Ataoja is the administrative and spiritual head of the town.

Osun still influences the decisions of the king, chiefs, priests and the economy of Osogbo each day. Individually, the people of Osogbo honor her daily in words and deeds. She promotes communal harmony among the Osogbo people. She also promotes harmony among divinities, Osogbo leadership and the people of Osogbo.

2. The Leadership of Osun: The constant communication that goes on between the earthly and spiritual beings, as we have seen with Osun, makes serving divinities a necessity for the traditional Yoruba people. It has been said that as the goddess of fertility, she cares for all the living in Osogbo (Deidre 1995: 68). Her involvement in the affairs of the community demonstrates that women are powerful in keeping men and women together in peace and harmony.

As we have seen earlier, Osun is one of the early divinities known in Yoruba language as *irunmole*, the mysterious beings. She is the last of the divinities,

> Even though Osun was the last of the seventeen odu (or orisa) who came to earth at the time of creation, she quickly became the most

> influential one by demonstrating to the remaining orisa that without her *ase* (power of life force), their mission could not succeed. Osun is probably this same olori-ikin, otherwise known as the wife of Orunmila in the context of the initiation of Ifa priests at Igbo du (the Ifa grove) (Abiodun 2001: 28).

Some other Yoruba divinities who are involved in the creation of the Yoruba world and people are Ogun, Orunmila, Obatala and Iyemoja (Omoyajowo 1975). Collectively, their mission on earth is to organize the earth and to rule over the affairs of people and the spiritual worlds. The occasional and annual sacrifices such as the Osun festival are significant to the Yoruba people in Osogbo (Clark 1966: 119). For each divinity values the specialization of the counterparts in maintaining orderliness in the Yoruba community.

A couple of the Yoruba divinities are women. Osetura in Ifa oracle states that Osun is one of the female divinities with charismatic ability and supernatural power that all Yoruba people honor throughout the world (Bascom 1943: 127-128). She represents womanhood (Denzer 1998). At one time, the rest of *Irunmole* "divinities" ignorantly overlooked her importance in fulfilling their mission on earth. In the first of their earlier meetings, they did not invite Osun. They intentionally violated the principle of equality that Olodumare required of them all. This particular meeting ended in dispute.

The male divinities went back to Olodumare to inquire about the reason for the failure of their meeting (Abiodun 2001: 16). Olodumare then asked as to the whereabouts of Osun, their sister. The divinities stated that she had not been invited to the meeting. Olodumare rebuked them for discriminating against her and he made them realize that each of them is equally important in keeping world peace.

To appease Osun, Olodumare asked the male divinities to apologize to her and to offer her sacrifices with an apology saying, "Mother, the preeminent hair-plaiter with the coral-beaded comb. We have been to the creator and it was there we discovered that all Odu were derived from you [Osun], and that our suffering would continue if we failed to recognize and obey you [Osun]." (Abiodun 2001: 17). This must have been a slap in the face for them because, in the Yoruba leadership, men rarely apologize to women in Yoruba myths. It was like asking an older person to publicly apologize to a younger person. Osun did not want to talk to other divinities. As Osun was about to curse them, Ose, a lesser divinity, covered Osun's mouth not to do so (Abiodun 2001: 18).

Among the Yoruba divinities, Osun has a special mission for the world. She has power over fertility. She can cure sickness and disease. She has control over still-birth and hears the cry of the oppressed. Today, as it was then, Osun monitors the activities of *aje* known as witches (Deidre 1995: 170). She recognizes and regulates the activities of *aje* (Adedeji 1967: 65). People appeal to Osun to forestall the threats of *aje* over themselves and their relatives (Deidre 1995: 172). Osun has the ability to distort the plans of other divinities especially Esu, who do not comply with the cosmic and social orders (Deidre 1995: 77). She believes in the peaceful co-existence of the divinities (Deidre 1995: 73).

Osun does not favor injustice among the Yoruba. Osun is one of the deities that wards off the evil activities of witches and sickness in the community. She constantly fights the enemies of her devotees. She represents her clients in the matter of their welfare, and pleads their case before other divinities. Barrenness, accidents, premature death nightmares and wars are some of the evils that Yoruba people fear. As gods and ancestors have power over Yoruba communities, so do demons, principalities and familiar spirits. Supernatural powers can be malevolent or benevolent, offend or defend people in the community (Ajayi and Smith 1964: 1).

Osun is the head of *aje* "witches" (Beier 1977: 16). *Aje* can turn human and natural events to their advantage, but Osun makes sure that justice prevails in Osogbo. For protection against evil, women are encouraged to bring their children to the annual festival to pray and offer sacrifices.

3. Osun, the Goddess of Fertility: Osun is continuously recreating lives, or at least giving children to barren families. Osun's source of power is Olodumare. All other divinities derive their special power from Olodumare too. Osun has a special power of granting children to women. Having a child is a necessity in Yorubaland. In the spirit world, Osun must release unborn babies to the earth. Any family that needs children often consults the priests to appease Osun.

Having power over fertility and protection gives Osun honor in the history of Yoruba people. As a mother, she was a pretty woman and a symbol of beauty. She was one of the wives of Sango. The concept of beauty in Yoruba is of two dimensions: the inward beauty and outward beauty. The latter is less significant than the former; to Yoruba people inward beauty is the most desirable. It is called *iwa lewa,* meaning character or right attitude. The test of the aesthetic is more of action, inaction and reaction in all circumstances (Lawal 1974: 239). In Yoruba's eyes, appearance is deceptive but character is more desired in a lady. Character is like smoke; it always reveals itself. For a Yoruba person, black is beautiful, but a fairly light person is more admirable, yet one's attitude matters most (Castellanons 2001: 35). Some think that showering regularly can lighten the complexion. For this reason some of her devotees think Osun is light in complexion because she is a goddess of a river.

In Yoruba belief, no matter how beautiful a lady might be, not getting a husband is a shame for her and her family. Osun was married to two husbands. At one time, she was married to Sango and in other myths she married Orunmila. It was unheard of in Yoruba culture for a woman to marry two husbands at the same time (Bascom 1942: 37). It can happen after divorce or the death of the husband. Marrying another member of her husband's family is called "*supo*" levirate. Levirate is a situation when a widow re-marries from the same kinship of her deceased husband. A brother of the dead husband is expected to marry his brother's widow (Bascom 1942: 39). In the circumstances where the man declines the marriage, the option would be declared open for anybody else in the family. In the case of Osun's marriages, how she had two husbands cannot be explained in Yoruba thought. The myths concerning this have simply been accepted.

Osun was one of the wives of Sango, the god of thunder (Deidre 1995: 48, 70-73). Sango was at one time the *Alafin* of Oyo (the king of Oyo), one of the super-power kingdoms in Yorubaland (Bascom 1944: 3, 7). Osun became his favorite wife (Farrow 1996: 51). The polygamy system is common practice in the Yoruba community, even today (Bascom 1942: 38).

4. Osun's Womanhood: Osun had firsthand experience of polygamy. Osun faced rivalry with other women at her husband's house (Deidre 1995: 48, 70-73). In addition to marrying Osun, Sango had other wives (Awolalu 1996: 34). When home became unbearable for Osun, she left Sango. This is what a polygamous family faces everyday. A Yoruba husband may ask his wife to go back to her parents if she becomes difficult. At her parents home such women are ridiculed by other women. Such "undisciplined" wives are called *adelebo* or *ilemosu* meaning "one who has disgracefully returned home." The *adelebo* or *ilemosu's* at the parents' home are threats to spinsters in the community. Competition for husbands becomes higher, and spinsters think that the *ilemosu* would hinder their chances to get husbands.

Osun's marriage to Sango attests to her royal lineage as a queen in her time, but she was not the only queen in the palace. Her rivals were *Oya* (the River Niger's goddess) and *Oba* (goddess of river) (Parrinder 1951/1976: 97). The three wives never got along in Sango's palace (Bascom 1944: 3).

Osun and Sango moved away from the palace. Osun moved to Osogbo (Farrow 1996: 51). The Yoruba people love to migrate from city to city either for trade or hunting (Deidre 1995: 158). Yoruba myths stated that Osun and Sango migrated for political reasons (Awolalu 1996: 34). One myth indicates that Sango's mother came from Nupe and conquered Oyo Empire where he possibly met Osun. This incident might be after the Nupe people encroached on the Oyo Empire, the old capital of Yorubaland (Deidre 1995: 158). Both Shango and Osun stayed for a short time in Oyo before they eventually moved on to Osogbo.

Oya and Oba did not get along very well in the polygamous setting. Due to the constant fights and misunderstandings at home, Shango divorced Osun and Oya (Awolalu 1996: 36; Schiltz 1985). He allowed each of his wives to go their separate ways. In Yoruba myths Osun, Oya and Oba became major rivers in Yoruba towns and villages. Osun is in Osogbo while, the Oba River flows between the boundary of Osogbo and Ibadan. Oya is the goddess of another major river. Oya is specially known as the River Niger, one of the biggest rivers in Nigeria. Apparently, all of Sango's wives control the Yorubaland rivers. The Yoruba cherish these goddesses by immortalizing them in their history. The Yorubas believe that parents immortalize themselves through childbearing, but gods and goddesses are turned into spiritual objects at death as memorials for their worshippers. And the most powerful men and women could physically turn themselves into natural things such as trees, wells, mountains, valleys and statues as well. Each of these claimed events and rumors often becomes an historical landmark in the life and mind of the people in the community.

5. Osun the Diviner: We have seen that Sango had more than one wife and Osun also had more than one husband. Osun married Orunmila and Sango (Deidre 1995: 70-73). Orunmila is the spiritual head of the divination services in Yoruba cities. Up until this moment, Orunmila's disciples are spiritual consultants for Yoruba people called '*babalawo*'.

The babalawo are narrators of Yoruba myths, tales and proverbs. Each day, they use these oracles in their practice of divination. The babalawo's main goal is to understand, devise and discern spiritual matters behind their clients' problems through the casting of cowries. The problems can be spiritual, emotional or physical. It is for the *babalawo* to consult the spirit world. As herbalists in the community, they know the language and minds of the people, the spirits, gods and goddesses. With herbalists wide knowledge of incantations, leaves, roots, animals, water and soil, they can move the hands of Yoruba gods and goddess to vindicate people's enemies and to cure their problems (Awolalu 1996: 69). Such priests are also philosophers. They are trained to find the cause and effect of the challenges facing clients. They rationalize, criticize and recommend sacrifices for the cure of the different diseases and illnesses.

Babalawo are diviners also. They are skillful narrators of Yoruba myths too. Even where some verses have been lost in transmission, they have access to special revelations through sacrifice to regain the verses from the divinities. For a babalawo, their interpretations and mythological knowledge must be up-to-date.

The babalawo are the students of Orunmila, and Orunmila is a husband of Osun. Osun assists her husband to make home a welcoming place for her husband's students. A well-fed and focused babalawo can predict the future through the divination. The instruments of divination are *opele* 'divination string,' *obi* 'kolanuts,' *opon-ifa* 'divination tray,' and *ofo* 'incantations.'

> OPELE is the name of a lesser oracle, who is regarded as a messenger of Ifa. He is represented by eight small laths of wood, and as it is a far easier task to consult him, the babalawos do each day, and in all lesser causes; but Ifa must be consulted every fifth day (Yoruba reckoning). The orishas Oshun, Yemaja, and Oshosi are consulted by their devotees, and so is Eshu (Elegbara), the evil spirit, whose answer is never disregarded (Farrow 1996: 42).

Divination is a lucrative spiritual calling in Yorubaland. There are a number of babalawo in each community. They are as common as pharmacists in the west. Every one of them has materials for divination. A divination tray, for instance, is one of the essential materials of Ifa oracles. This tray contains soil, spread even on it, where divination codes are written and decoded through the assistance of *Orunmila,* the mythological father of Yoruba divination. These codes are shorthand writings of what the *Babalawo* hear from the heavens, and which are temporarily written down on the tray for further explanation for the clients. The plates are the properties of the wife. Plates that westerners would consider household materials are what the Yoruba people would think of as having supernatural and spiritual origins and consequences (Bascom 1981: 15). People's attitude towards the diviner is critical, based on the effectiveness of their performance and how knowledgeable they are in Yoruba myths (Bascom 1981: 15).

It is appropriate to understand the roles of babalawo "diviners" to see why Osun is often remembered among the Yoruba (Bascom 1981: 15). The father of all babalawo is Orunmila, the husband of Osun. She knows her husband's thoughts and deeds more than anybody, apart from *Olodumare.*

Orunmila plans the Osun festival with his *ifa*, Yoruba oracles. Ifa has sixteen major parts called *oju odu* and two hundred and forty sub-sections called *omo odu* (Olabimtan 1974: 50). The *Babalawo* uses *odu-ifa* as *oral tools* for making voodoo powers, charms, anti-demons medicine *oyeku*. Odu-ifa are instruments of incantations *ofo* and commands *afose*. The combination of the *odu-ifa* 'ifa oracles' is called *ofo* 'incantation'. No two *ofo* 'incantations' are the same, for babalawo usually claim that they receive the revelation of the verses fresh from Orunmila, their father and teacher.

Anybody who wants to be a *babalawo* "priest" has to spend years under Orunmila and Osun's domain. As Orunmila knows his disciples so also does Osun. She knows the *odu-ifa* 'ifa oracles', *ofo* 'incantations' and *ebo* "sacrifices" far better than her husband's apprentices. The men and women who work directly with Osun believe that they have a deeper knowledge of Yoruba medicine than the *babalawo* "priests" who ignore her. Whenever *ofo* and *afose* are recited, people claim they experience the miraculous touch of ancestors, gods and goddesses.

The *babalawo* are also fortune-tellers, future-tellers and palm-readers. Osun, as a wife of the father of the *Babalawo*, could also provide these services to her devotees (Deidre 1995: 57). The Yoruba worldview is very spiritual, and one needs to be fully equipped with *oogun* "charms" to survive. The more *oogun* "charms" one has, the more powerful one is in the community. Osun is one of the sources of power for the Yoruba people. They use this power for religious and political gain in the community.

Osun has enormous spiritual power to share with her devotees. Whenever necessary *Baale-ile* offers a sacrifice (*ru ebo*) to Osun to reeive power and protection for the members of the family. Often, each family has a shrine that "represents the face of divinities in the family" (Thorpe 1991:100). Human beings and deities regularly meet at religious centers for worship. This use of religious symbols and obligations keeps the memory of divinities afresh in peoples' minds (Warner-Lewis 1999: 22).

Orunmila, the husband of Osun, gives each family a list of materials for sacrifice. Babalawo "the priest" acts as an intermediary between Orunmila and each family. Through consultation with Ifa, Orunmila decides the date and materials to be used for the Osun sacrifice. Each item of the sacrifice has a religious meaning for the time.

6. Osun as a Mother: It is very difficult to get information on Osun and Orunmila's marriage historically. But Yoruba myths say that Osun cures infertility of womanhood and that power accorded her the honor of being called the mother of the barrens. It is a common practice to call the divinity who answers the prayers of the barren people "a mother". The *ifa* oracle verses state that Osun usually appeased Orunmila to cure women of their infertility (Deidre 1995: 84).

Osun knew the agony of being barren and the joy of being a mother because for some time in her marriage she was without a child (Bascom 1943: 128). The '*ese ifa*' Ifa verses said that Osun wanted to have children badly (Deidre 1995: 82). She contacted three *ifa* priests and her husband's former students for prescriptions to cure the barrenness. The names of these students are: Efin, Duro and Ojiyaomefun. They are the ones who assisted her in curing her barrenness. This story also suggests that divinities are not all-powerful. One divinity often depends on another divinity to fulfill their destiny.

Osun's children were mythological children because she has a productive power. Barren men and women, most especially women, often approach Osun for children. When they have children, these children are known as *omo Osun* "Osun's children." Osun's invaluable role in the production, reproduction and protection of children is cherished by the Yoruba (Bascom 1942:41). Even at the other side of the Atlantic Ocean, Osun still cares for her "children" (Diedre 1995: 89). She is actively involved in reproduction as she gives her devotees the water of life (Beier 1977: 7, 20). Any barren women who drink from her water become pregnant. Obatala, as her co-divinity, moulds human images and puts them in Osun's womb (Lawal 1974: 242-243; Clark 1966: 119). Every human being born in Yorubaland has to pass through Osun's womb (Deidre 1995: 81). Osun is said to be a very beautiful person and all her children to be beautiful in character and in appearance. For the Yoruba, outward and inward beauties mirror the sacredness of the divinity (Beier 1977: 11, 52).

Osun's fertility is an important subject in keeping her history alive in the Yoruba community. It is a joy to have a child who would inherit one's possessions. A Yoruba proverb says *"omo niyun, omo ni ide"* which connotes the idea that "having a child is like having a collection of jewels, or precious gold" (Bamgbose 1968: 80-86). Osun had great wealth, she is called "a wealthy woman who has a golden (brass) mortar," but her joy at being a mother made her important to the community (Diedre 1995: 82).

Osun is a hard-working mother. As mothers provide for and protect their children, Osun cares for her too. One of the Yoruba sayings states that *"Baba ni baba gbogbo aye"* "father belongs to all the children" in a polygamous family. This proverb indicates that each mother is responsible for the well-being of her own biological children in such a setting.

Osun protects her children with all her power. She protects her children from the most fearful group of killers known as *aje* "witches". Osun is the leader of *aje* witches (Diedre 1995: 73-74). Osun does not condone injustice therefore she punishes the wicked *aje* who do "havoc over the children or their parents" (Diedre 1995: 170). Any *aje* who kill children indiscriminately in the community are publicly mocked by the people (Adedeji 1967: 66, 67). This belief has enhanced the moral standards of the community. Nobody can hide under the influence of spiritual power to perpetrate evil on innocent people.

Osun acts on behalf of Olodumare, to promote peace and harmony in the community (Diedre 1995: 77). Osun removes her protection from anybody who allows *Esu* "devil" to use her against the innocents. Osun maintains checks-and-balances in justice and equity among the people. Leadership, responsibility and accountability are closely linked in the Yoruba community. In short, Osun proves herself to be a mother who possesses a spiritual force over human and spiritual beings (Murphy and Sanford 2001: 6). She is responsible for protecting not only children but also pregnant women from an untimely death (Cannon 1942: 180; Diedre 1995: 89). Miscarriages are not treated as normal occurrences for women. A spirit or a person is thought to be the cause of it (Diedre 1995: 76).

D. Osogbo: Osun's Original Setting

Osogbo is not only an important Yoruba town but its location gives us more information about the history of the Osun festival and its continuity. Osogbo is where six major Yoruba roads meet. These roads connect Osogbo to Ile-Ife, Ilesha, Ekiti, Ilorin and Oyo. Osogbo is located approximately 96 kilometers northeast of Ibadan, another big Yoruba town. The majority of Yoruba in the cities mentioned above recognize the divine status of Osun.

Geographically, Osogbo is situated on latitude 7.7 degree and longitude 4.5 degree east. It is located in a tropical forest region of today's Yorubaland. The River Osun is a major source of water for people and animals. There are two major seasons in Yorubaland, the rainy and the dry seasons. During the rainy season, Osogbo has an average monthly rainfall of about 0.6 meters. Like most of the Yoruba cities and towns, Osogbo's vegetation is a tropical forest. The north of Osogbo, especially towards Ikirun town is grassland that provides pasture for cattle-rearing. In those days, Osogbo connected with the Oba River, sharing boundaries with the Ibadan people. On the northern boundary of Osogbo is Ikirun (Parrinder 1951/1976: 97). As we have seen, in our discussion Osogbo is a major Yoruba town (Parrinder 1951/1976: 73) and it is significant in trying to understand the Yoruba people, culture and religion. Osogbo people are friends of Ilesa and the Ibadan people.

1. Yoruba Meets Osun
So far we have seen Osun as a wife, mother and protector of children. She has her footprints in the history of sacred spots in Osogbo. No other female divinity can claim or contest Osun's leadership among the male-dominated culture and religious setting of Osogbo. The origins of Osogbo would be helpful in understanding Osun myths.

In our efforts to understand the links that connect the Yoruba people to Osun and Osogbo, we need to examine the history behind it. In the beginning, Yoruba people were a nomadic tribal group, but around 1700, they settled down in the southwestern portion of what is today called Nigeria (Matibag 1996: 52). From there, the Yoruba as a people started spreading to all over West Africa (Warner-Lewis 1999: 19). In one of the earliest records of Yoruba history, Eugenio said, "the Yoruba of the Guinea Coast do not comprise a single "tribe" but rather consist of numerous and varied tribal groups only loosely unified by [a] common language, mythology, history, dress, and ritual symbolism" (Matibag 1996: 51). The loosely unified elements are clearly seen in their languages, religious activities and customs today. These elements are even obvious in the Yoruba people of various distinct local areas: the Egba, Egbado, Awori, Ijebu, Ijesha, Oyo, Owo, Ife, Ondo and many more groups within a similar group (Herskovits 1966: 218). Each of these groups speaks the Yoruba language with a distinct accent from their neighbor. Occasionally, the differences in Yoruba ethnic accents are so strong that Yoruba-Awori may not comprehend what Yoruba-Egbado is saying, despite the fact that their languages have the same vocabulary. The Yoruba people in Oyo or from Oyo normally claim to be the "Yoruba proper," likewise other Yoruba groups contend this exclusive claim (Matibag 1996: 51). No doubt, historically the origin of all Yoruba people is Ile-Ife while Oyo is the military headquarters of Yoruba people. Osogbo is known as the headquarters of Osun worship (Matibag 1996: 52; Frobenius 1913). Today, Osogbo is still one of the big towns in Yorubaland. In 1991, Osun became one of the states in the Federal Republic of Nigeria (Awe and Albert 1995: v). Osun as a goddess has now found her place in the history of Nigeria (Diedre 1995: 53).

i. The First Myth: Ilesa was first founded in an area not far from Osogbo. From Ilesa many smaller groups of people moved out to establish their own independent communities. Osogbo is one of the little communities that emerged from Ilesa. Timehin and Ogidan, two of the leading hunters, left the boundaries of Ilesa on the command of Olarooye (Awe and Albert 1995: 3). Timehin, the chief hunter, and his people experienced two mysterious events. First, Timehin found an elephant by the riverside, and he shot and killed it. He then tied the dead elephant to a tree. The spot where the event happened is called *Idi Ogun* "Ogun Shrine". The second experience was that these people found the source of a big river. They thought within themselves that this would be a pleasant place for their people to relocate their families. As a marker for this historical finding, Timehin felled the trees around the area. As the trees were falling down, he claimed to have heard a female voice shouting *Ta lo fo ikoko aro mi, eyin Oso-Igbo tun de o* meaning "who broke my indigo pots, you wizards of the forest are here again!" Osogbo" is the contracted form of *"Oso Igbo"* (Spirit of the Forest). Here is how Olupona

summarized the Yoruba myth:
> According to this myth history, Osogbo was founded by a prince of Ilesa, a Yoruba city state about 20 kilometers from Osogbo. Prince Olarooye (Larooye) had settled in a village called Iponle, near Ilesa. As a result of a water shortage in Iponle, Olarooye and Olutimehin (Timehin), a hunter, led a group of people in search of water, as was the custom in ancient days. The duo and their cohorts discovered a large river, later called Osun. They went back to report to Owate, Olarooye's father, and to invite Owate to settle in the new place on the Osun riverbank. But before they left, they decided to make a mark on the riverbank where they discovered Osun. They felled a big tree that made a very loud noise on the river, whereupon they heard a loud booming voice say: *Won ti wo ikoko aro mi o eyinn Oso inu igbo e tun de* (You have destroyed my pots of dyes. You wizard of the forest, you're here again) (Olupona 2001: 49).

On hearing the cry, Timehin and Ogidan were terrified. They knew that they were trespassing on spiritual ground. As the voice identified herself as Osun, the two people responded to the voice that they had come in peace and they explained their mission. Osun then asked Timehin and Ogidan to lead their people from Iponle to resettle around her domain (Awe and Albert 1995: 3).

As a result of this historical encounter with Osun, the name of the spot started to be called "Osogbo" as it was derived from the voice they heard saying *Oso Igbo ni mi* translating as "I am the wizard of the forest" (Centre for African Settlement Studies and Development 1993: 11). Since then the people began to address themselves as Osogbo people, the contraction form of the phrase *oso igbo*. As a respect for the kind gesture of Osun in accommodating the Iponle immigrants, the people inaugurated an annual religious festival in her honor known as the Osun festival. The Osun festival, therefore, is a historical festival that marks the beginning of a town in Yorubaland.

In the Yoruba praise-worship *"oriki,"* Osogbo's development and expansion was said to be rapid because many immigrants fled from different villages and towns to settle there (Diedre 1995: 158). The Osun festival is an annual reminder for the descendants of the settlers. It is a celebration of the social-political history of Osogbo. It is an occasion when both spiritual and religious leaders gather to acknowledge the kindness of Osun (Osogbo Cultural Heritage Council 1994: 16; Diedre 1995: 53).

As the people settled down, they got to know more about Osun's personality. Later they learned that Osun was the wife of Sango, the god of thunder and lightning (Diedre 1995: 48, 70-73). Sango's marriage with Osun attested to her status as one of the divinities. Osun became a role model for the ladies in Yorubaland. Sango's mother came from Nupe and conquered Oyo Empire, while Osun came from Ijumu and settled in Osogbo (Diedre 1995: 81; Johnson and Johnson).

ii. The Second Myth: Another myth indicates that the origin of Osogbo was directly tied to the Yoruba divinities and the founding of Ile-Ife, the Garden of Eden of the Yoruba people (Murphy and Sanford 2001:1; Abimbola 1975: 157-197). Osun was one of the *orisa* "divinities" who descended from heaven to Ile-Ife (Diedre 1995: 160). Ile-Ife is considered to be where the universe begins. For many centuries, Ile-Ife was the historic administrative headquarters of all Yoruba people, villages, towns and cities.

As male divinities were moving out of Ile-Ife to lead different towns of Yoruba kingdom, at one time, Osun left Ile-Ife to provide leadership for the people of Osogbo. This myth is more credible because Osogbo is located about 60 kilometers away from Ile-Ife. The Osun annual festival started to mark the spiritual and political leadership of Osun as one of the Yoruba divinities. This annual festival contributes to the growth and expansion of Osogbo as one of the Yoruba towns. Osogbo is not a mythological place in time and space. It is a pilgrimage city for the devotees of Osun.

iii. The Third Myth: The third version of how Osogbo started was written by Deji Olugunna in 1959 (Olugunna 1959: 12-16). Contrary to the mythological versions above, Olaro-Oye who was the seventh king of Iponle, founded Osogbo. He was a descendant of Ajibogun, the son of Owa of Ilesha (Olugunna 1959: 9-10). Iponle Omu or Iponle town was a suburb settlement not far from Ilesha. Osogbo is about eight kilometers away from Iponle. Although, today, Iponle is smaller than Osogbo, but Iponle is older than Osogbo. Olaro-Oye is the same person as Larooye, and Laro.

A poem says the king is: OMO IJESA OGUNRALU, OMO ARINLOSIN, GADEWOLU ATAOJA AKOKO L'ODE OSOGBO" (Osogbo Cultural Heritage Council 1994: 27). The king of Iponle, Olaro Oye or Larooye who was the seventh king of the place, was the first to bear the title of Ataoja the present official tittle of Osogbo's king. He and some of the Iponle people migrated to Osogbo as they were searching for a water supply. The small community relocated near the Osun River, a pleasant and better place for water supply and a place to continue their farming (Diedre 1995: 81; Abimbola 1975: 157). With gratitude, the immigrants inaugurated the annual worship of Osun.

Timehin, a hunter by profession, who was a brother of Olaro-oye, was appointed as the head of the hunters, which is like a commander-in-chief of the army (Awe and Albert 1995: 2). Olaro-oye became the chief-priest of Osun (Ojo 1969: 164; Fadipe: 199). Gradually, people from different parts of the known world migrated to Osogbo is search of a better future. Osun was recognized as the goddess of the land (Diedre 1995: 106).

One of the Yoruba songs of praise states that Osun is the "source of water" (Murphy and Sanford 2001: 1). Cities surrounded by rivers are safer during inter-tribal wars. Naturally, the Yoruba people migrated in search of business, security, and always look for opportunities. Historically, during wars, *Olumo* Rock was a refuge for the Egba, and Osun River was a barrier against the enemies of Osogbo people (Diedre 1995: 159). Its water did not dry up during the dry season, and the enemies could not penetrate the city during wars (Ojo 1966).

One of the disadvantages of settling at a river bank is the threat of flood that they experience once in a while without warning. Rather than being scared of the Osun River, people bring offerings and sacrifices regularly to the river-bank. Physically, the river became a line of defense for the community. Spiritually, the people believe that Osun is their protector, their defense against natural and supernatural forces that have been part of Yoruba military and religious concerns (Ajayi and Smith 1964: 1). Individuals and the community are always looking for natural and supernatural reinforcement. As it has been said, this desire led the Iponle people to migrate close to their goddess, Osun.

This closeness to the river claimed many lives and property. During one of the rainy seasons, Osogbo was flooded and buildings and farms were washed away (Centre for African Settlement Studies and Development 1993: 5-11). The people often rushed to the conclusion that Osogbo was flooded because somebody in the community had offended her. The next thing they did was to consult the Ifa oracles and offered sacrifices to appease Osun (Awe and Albert 1995: 2). It is claimed that during such sacrifices, a very big fish, representing the gods of the Osun River known as Iko, normally emerged from the river (Centre for African Settlement Studies and Development 1993: 11). Its appearance was a sign of a good omen for the people and the town. The religious significance of Osun gave Osogbo a wide recognition in Yoruba kingdom, especially in the towns and villages that relied on Osun for their water supply.

2. Myths in the Yoruba Belief

Adedeji has once said, "that Yoruba myths and contents are designed to maintain the social fiber of a traditional community" (Adedeji 1967: 64). From such observation, Benjamin Ray proposed the importance of myths in explaining the origin of human beings as:

> Most African myths deal primarily with the origin of man and with the origin of certain social and ritual institutions that account for real-life situations. These myths explain the basic conditions of human life as the people now find it. For this reason, African mythology contains a good deal of what we would call "history." Indeed, in African oral tradition 'myth' and 'history' generally overlap and shade into one another. Myth blends into history as cosmic and archetypal events bear upon local situations, and history blends into a myth as local and human events become ritualized and infused with cosmic and archetypal meaning (Ray 2000: 24).

Myths answer some of the common questions of life. Myths are helpful in building religious beliefs for a community and people can see the relevance of myths in day-to-day religious practices (Diedre 1995:48). Yoruba myths show that the "histories of humans, their societies, cultures, and religions do not begin only at the moment they [are written down] become literate and from which historians can produce their histories" (Platvoet 1996: 46). African religion, in particular, relies heavily on myths and festivals to recreate events of the beginning. Myths come alive in religious festivals and foster their continuation in different parts of the world. During religious festivals, different versions of myths are brought together as one in celebration. In the Osun festival, for instance, there are more than five different versions of myths that explain the origin of Osogbo.

Yoruba myths, for instance, contain people's names and places thus making them historically credible. These myths are retold day-by-day until the community members have memorized them. In this way, myths create a sense of reverence and awe in the minds of the community in their world of imagination. Myths enhance community historical speculations and reinforce people's quest for reality. Myths become more believable when one considers how frequent they are points of reference and the numbers of divinities that are involved in the stories.

The Yoruba people celebrate the different versions of myths in religious festivals. The multiplicity of myths enhances the beauty of festivals and the practice of religion. However, the intention of religious festivals is not to make converts of others, but to celebrate unity in diversity. It has been said that the intention of myths is "not (to) assume that we have to save the world, not even the Yoruba world" (Beier 1977: 6). In other words, the celebration of the mythological gods in religious festivals is not intended for competition or converting people into any particular religious worship.

Myths contain religious ideas, beliefs, symbols, attitudes, sentiments, practices, and thoughts useful for present and future generations. The African lifestyle is built upon locally integrated myths (Adedeji 1971: 135). Its continuation reinforces the survival of the myths as well (Bascom 1967: 52). Myths are therefore important in understanding the history of African religion. Scholars have made genuine efforts to establish the historical values of African religion through myths. Some useful ideas on myths from a non-African continent like Ranger and Kimambo 1972 study is valuable to this study (see also Badejo 1995: 13). Here, the idea is to particularly illuminate on Yoruba myths as a way to understand a Yoruba festival in the context of Osun in Osogbo.

3. Historical Explanations of the Origin of Osun

Samuel Johnson, a reverend father who served in Yorubaland, claimed that Osogbo was established in around the seventeenth century during the reign of Alaafin Kori of the Oyo Empire (Johnson and Johnson 1970: 156). Kori was the fifth Alaafin of Oyo at the time (Diedre 1995: 156). The king wanted to quench some insurrections that were hindering the expansion of the Oyo Empire southward. Some individuals and groups were constantly harassing traders as they traveled from Ijebu to do business at Apomu market, a very prosperous Yoruba town. The towns and villages that were being affected jointly secured the military assistance of Oyo, the military headquarters of the Yoruba. Hence, Alaafin Kori established a military post at Ede, which eventually grew into the city known today as Ede (Diedre 1995: 156). On behalf of the Oyo Empire, the group of hunters dealt with the opposition groups.

In a reaction to the Oyo Empire's action, the Owa of Ilesa also established a rival political station near Ede which eventually developed into a city that is today known as Osogbo (Awe and Albert 1995: 2). Owa, the king of Ilesa, established this station to reject the Alafin's authority and expansion toward her region. Owa of Ilesa then appointed a vassal king, the Atewogbeja of Osogbo, to rule the station (Johnson and Johnson 1921: 156). Eventually, Osogbo became an independent Yoruba city that stopped the expansion of Oyo authority southward. The only authority figure that Ilesa and Osogbo recognized was Ile-Ife, the political headquarters of Yoruba kingdom. All this happened at the time when Ile-Ife and Oyo were contesting for authority over all other towns and villages in the Yoruba kingdom. In support of this storyline, a praise-worship song *"oriki-orile"* of Osun suggests that many immigrants fled their villages, for safety when Ile-Ife and Oyo Empires were contending the Yoruba Kingdom (Diedre 1995: 158).

All these myths are retold during the Osun festival as the people celebrate the political and spiritual leaders' involvement in founding of the city (Diedre 1995: 53, 63). From the beginning of Osogbo, Yoruba leaders managed and controlled the political, economic, religious, and social institutions of the place (Paltvoet 1996: 51). As Osogbo was an offshoot of Ilesa, the Ilesa people still respect their historical involvement in Osogbo developments (Awe and Albert 1995: 3). Ilesa, Ile-Ife and Osogbo respect Osun for helping one of their own during difficult times (Olugunna 1959). Osogbo leaders are direct descendants of Ajibogun, the son of oba "king" of Ilesa (Awe and Albert 1995: 3). There are other factors that contributed to the growth of Osogbo and the recognition of the roles of Osun in Osogbo. Whichever story one believes, mythological or historical, Osogbo is a city for the refugees.

i. A Series of Inter-Tribal Wars: As we have mentioned, Osogbo was founded by a group of Yoruba immigrants from Ilesa. The people of Ilesa are called Ijesa. Some of the Ijesa migrated to the banks of a river which is today known as the Osun. There was a series of wars in Yorubaland in 1840. Osun assisted the citizens of Osogbo in winning the wars. Osogbo became the *Oroki Asala,* "this connotes that no matter the pressing situation, any one who escaped into Osogbo was sure of safety and protection" (Osogbo Cultural Heritage Council 1994: 16).

On various occasions, the Osogbo faced wars with the Fulani jihadists who were Muslims from the northern part of the country. From the southwest direction, the Dahomey invaded them from time to time. During one of the attacks, Osun changed into a woman, and she sold vegetables to the Fulani warriors. After eating the vegetables, the Fulani soldiers had loosened bowels and lost their energy to fight (Beier 1977: 20; Ajayi and Smith 1964: 33). To keep their memories of this victory fresh, the people sing songs that ridicule the efforts of the Fulani during the annual festival.

One historian recorded the attack as follows: "From the west, Dahomey recently freed from Oyo control, began to strive to expand into Yorubaland and, until close to the end of the century, repeatedly invaded western Yoruba territories" (Parrinder 1951/1976: xvii). The attacks were motivated by a desire to gain independence from the Oyo Empire.

In the course of these battles, especially between 1817 and 1893, the Oyo kingdom fought and conquered the Fon of Dahomey, a non-Yoruba neighboring tribe. Most of the town and villages in Dahomey came under the control of the Oyo Empire (Verger 1976: 459).

> Big cities are known to control the small villages and towns in Yorubaland. It has been said that, the rise of [in the] number of successor states to the Oyo Empire notably Ibadan, Ijaye, new Oyo, and Abeokuta – in the former territories of the Owu and Egba, and the rivalry between them to inherit the former political position of the Alafins led to a new and prolonged series of wars. Also, some older kingdoms, like Ijebu and Ife, now tried to expand vigorously. For instance, Ife encroached on the towns of its southern neighbour, Ondo, and thereby set up a chain of disastrous events in that forest country (Parrinder 1951/1976: xvii).

During the said wars, Osogbo was caught between the two strong Yoruba warring towns. Its location made it difficult to avoid taking sides in the battles among the Yoruba cities. Eventually, Osogbo became the best ally of the Ibadan people. They mutually supported each other in battle against their common enemies. It is recorded that "in 1840, the Ibadan army conquered the Ilorin army at Osogbo and drove them back to Ofa" (Parrinder 1951/1976: 3). This victory gave Ibadan more territorial power over the other competing Yoruba states. Ibadan became the recognized military kingdom in all Yorubaland. By 1870, Ibadan had successfully conquered Ife, Ilesa and Ekiti. The other Yoruba states felt Ibadan was a threat. In 1877, Ibadan, a friendly Yoruba town to Osogbo, now with the support of other Yoruba towns that she had defeated attacked the people of Egba and Ijebu (Parrinder 1951/1976: 3). Osogbo was indirectly involved in inter-tribal wars and the people of Osogbo relied on Osun for victory.

During the Yoruba wars, each Yoruba community solicited the supports of similar divinities and another town. We see such cooperation in Osogbo, Abeokuta and Ibadan victories over their enemies:

> The defeat of the Fulani of Ilorin at Oshogbo in about 1840, the successful repulse by Abeokuta of the Dahomi attack in 1851, the victory in a prolonged campaign of the Ibadan at Ijaye in 1861-2, and the victory of Ibadan over the Ilorin and their Yoruba allies at Ikirun in 1878 (Ajayi and Smith 1964: 32).

These are just the most recognized confrontations among the Yoruba communities in the land, but there were other battles that are only recorded in Yoruba myths. The European slave trade encouraged wars among the West African groups due to the demand of slaves in the developed worlds (Patterson 1982: 120). Many lives were lost as the local people were greedy for landed properties and territories.

The majority of those captured alive in battles ended up in the New World as slaves. European traders waited at the coastal towns of the Atlantic Ocean, to buy the captured Yoruba slaves. Thousands of Yoruba people were sold and transported to the New World. Unfortunately, Osogbo was one of the coastal cities that suffered at the hands of slave-traders and many of the people were carried away to the New World (Hugh 1997: 47). Some of these Yoruba people were familiar with Osun. This explained how Osun worship started as a religious cult in the Americas.

ii. The Colonial Influences: In addition to religious, cultural and immigration necessities that contributed to the origins of Osogbo, the coming of the British officers to the area had an impact on the growth of Osogbo (Osogbo Cultural Heritage Council 1994: 37). The British government adopted an indirect rule system of government in Nigeria. The British government worked with the kings in ruling the Yoruba people. The Yoruba kings who cooperated with them gained more recognition and support from the British government. Osogbo gained the British colonial government support and one of the early British stations was built at Osogbo. Between 1903 and 1917, Osogbo had the network of roads: Osogbo-Ilesa-Akure-Benin Road in 1909; Osogbo-Ikirun road in 1911, Osogbo-Ogbomosho road in 1912, and Osogbo-Ede road in 1913 (Osogbo Cultural Heritage Council 1994: 36). Osogbo eventually became one of their district headquarters in Nigeria.

Today, Osogbo is a developed town in Nigeria. It is 96 kilometers northeast of Ibadan. Over the years, Hausa descendants had migrated to Osogbo from the north of country because of the availability of green grass for their cattle. Osun serves as a source of water supply for their animals all year round. And the location is suitable for growing cash crops such as cocoa, banana, kolanut, cassava, orange, mango, rubber and corn. The early settlers made the right choice in moving to the present site of Osogbo.

iii. The Growth and Development of Osogbo: The rapid growth of Osogbo has contributed to its historical recognition in Yorubaland. Its inhabitants are known for welcoming other immigrants into their community. Osogbo is an economically viable intersection where six roads lead to other major Yoruba towns (Osogbo Cultural Heritage Council 1994: 14). These roads lead to Ile-Ife, Ilesa, Ekiti, Ilorin and Oyo, Iwo, Akure, Gbongan, Ibadan and many more. Osogbo's location became a network centre for most Yoruba business people. It is a pilgrimage centre for traditional worshippers (Diedre 1995: 157).

The Osun River serves as the source of water for the people of Osogbo and its environs. It is a good place to raise animals, and for doing different kinds of farming. Directly or indirectly, farmers in Ekiti, Ilesha and Ile-Ife, benefit from the water supply also, Yoruba farmers in the neighboring towns bring their products to Osogbo for sale. Traders from Ilorin bring cotton materials to *Oja oba* "the king's market" in Osogbo (Olugunna 1959: 23). Many of the people who initially visited Osogbo market for business eventually moved their families to Osogbo.

Another factor that contributed to the rapid growth of Osogbo was the presence of *Oja Larooye* Larooye Market. The importance of this site is that it became the business centre of Osogbo and for the neighboring cities (Osogbo Cultural Heritage Council, *Osun Osogbo Festival*: 9). Early settlers met every five days to trade their farm produce (Osogbo Cultural Heritage Council, *Osun Osogbo Festival*: 10). *Oke Ohuntoto* and Ojaa Larooye became popular commercial centers that attracted people to become permanent residents of the area (Osogbo Cultural Heritage Council 1994: 13).

In the early days, the Yoruba gave Osogbo a nickname *Ode Osogbo* "centre of Osogbo" (Osogbo Cultural Heritage Council, *Osun Osogbo Festival*: 13). This nickname reflects its welcoming atmosphere for people of different languages and backgrounds. The traditional chiefs used to assemble every Friday to deliberate on important issues affecting the people in the town (Osogbo Cultural Heritage Council, *Osun Osogbo Festival*: 13). At one time, they had to discuss the effects of floods on the city (Osogbo Cultural Heritage Council, *Osun Osogbo Festival*: 14). They saw the danger of floods and how Osun had "overflowed its banks destroying the buildings and carrying away in its deluge the property of the inhabitants" (Osogbo Cultural Heritage Council, *Osun Osogbo Festival*: 14). It was a community that had no social security benefits, no insurance, or life insurance. The only strength it had was the will to survive. Every natural disaster was attributed to supernatural beings. The people had to move to a higher ground at the recommendation of the priests.

The divine direction always served as guidelines for the people. Whenever there was imminent danger, the Ifa priests asked the town people to appease the Osun River with sacrifice of *agbo* (a ram), *yanrin* (a kind of spinach) and *egbo* (coked corn-meal) (Osogbo Cultural Heritage Council, *Osun Osogbo Festival*: 15). With such sacrifices, the relationship between the human beings and divinities were mended from time to time. In return, Osun would rise to the defence of her people by granting them peace and tranquility (Diedre 1995: 82). The priests helped the community a lot through divination and oracles (Diedre 1995: 13). These priests contributed in preserving people's lives in Osogbo. The priests, by consulting Osun through Ifa oracles, helped in the Osun festival (Diedre 1995: 54).

The monarchy has assisted the growth of Osogbo town and people's interest in Osun worship. The king is the political and spiritual head of Osogbo. Whatever he says is binding on his subjects that is why they say *toba lase* meaning "the one that has authority over all." With all this respect, the kings always honor the divinities in public festivals. The king of Osogbo honors Osun and his subjects follow his example (Murphy and Sanford 2001: 6). It is written:

> From Osogbo in Osun State to Ikoro in Ekiti, from Ibadan in Oyo to Ijumu in Kwara State of Nigeria, and throughout the Yoruba diaspora in the Caribbean, Latin America, and North America, the Yoruba continue to venerate their most powerful female orisa (deity), Osun. The images alluding to her presence and power are as diverse as the people and the geographical locations where she is worshiped. Thus, the definition of

Osun's identity extends beyond Osogbo and many Yoruba towns where she is believed to have turned into the Osun River, and where festivals are held in her honor annually (Abiodun 2001: 10).

This recognition is passed on orally to all the succeeding kings in the area (Diedre 1995: 15). Osun receives such honor from kings both in kind and cash. It has been said, "Osun imagery, the mysterious consummation of life is a power that humbles rulers and followers alike" (Diedre 1995). Kings are second to the divinities "*igba keji*" and one of these divinities is Osun. One of the ways this prestige is kept intact is that Yoruba kings are rarely seen in public. People see them during special and religious occasions. Men and women, young and old are accountable to the king and divinities. Ironically, Yoruba believe that the offence of one person could bring catastrophe on all in the community.

Osogbo is a peaceful and quiet city to live in. People obey the rule of law and are friendly to strangers. They follow peace and justice as laid down by the kingship and Osun. They fear the consequences of their actions or inactions, because Osun is watching their character and know their attitude. Osogbo has therefore become the city of immigrants "*atipo*" and the population is growing as people moved from other Yoruba towns (Centre for African Settlement Studies and Development 1993: 1). Osogbo is growing in popularity and in number of inhabitants.

The cultural and religious lessons of Osogbo are preserved in *ijala*, the hunters who entertained public audience during religious ceremonies (Babalola 1964: 47).

As the kingdom grew, the early settlers had to move a few meters away, from the river banks because of the threat of floods and expanded towards the *Oja Oba* (king's market) (Centre for African Settlement Studies and Development 1993: 11). The king's palace was relocated to be very close to the market, which gave him more control over the religious and economic activities of Osogbo. The first palace is located in the present Osun Court Yard, the second palace was name OKE OHUNTOTO which is now the a sacred shrine where Ogboni Cult members meet periodically, and the third palace was built where the Ikirun, Ilesa, Ibadan, Ilorin, Ogbomoso, and Ede footpath roads intersected (Osogbo Cultural Heritage Council 1994: 54-59).

Food crops are produced in large quantities in Osogbo. Osun's favorite food is *egbo* "corn meal." Whenever the people of Osogbo eat this Yoruba-made meal, they remember Osun. Some are of the opinion that the word "Osogbo" is taken from the same *egbo* "a corn meal" that Yoruba people like to eat. *Egbo* "corn meal" is made of dry corn or maize called *agbado*. The story states that many people in this particular side of Yorubaland love to deal with *egbo*, therefore they have *iso-egbo*, an *egbo* stand. Osogbo is a short form of *Iso-Egbo* "a market/store for the corn-meal." This corn porridge is a fast food for the travelers, so they named the place "Osogbo" the home of "*egbo*" specialists (Awe and Albert 1995: 3). *Egbo* "corn-meal" therefore is a part of the Osun sacrifice.

Osogbo has experienced various systems of government including monarchy, colonial, parliamentary, republic, and democratic governments. Gradually, the local and national government authorities gained wider authorities over the monarchy. By January 1966, the Osogbo District Council came into effect. The indigenous people of Osogbo elected local representatives for the Osogbo District Council who represented them in the Federal Government of Nigeria.

Under this new system of government the kings not only lost control over the people, but the Osogbo people became more liberal in the things of the spirit. Spiritual and dogmatic beliefs were challenged by education. Ataoja could only preside over the traditional, territorial, social and religious matters. In May 1973, the Management Council took over the legislative, judiciary and executive power of Osogbo.

Although the *Ataoja* temporarily lost some of his roles to the Local and Federal governments of Nigeria, Osun still retained her sovereignty over the religious, history and social systems of Osogbo. One of the Nigerian states, in the area of Osogbo, has been named as Osun State. Osun has got her place on the African and world map. The Osun festival is also gaining the recognition of the national government as they often send federal and state representatives to witness the festival. It is possible in the near future that the Osun festival will become a national public holiday.

We have explained that Osogbo is the city of Osun and she is directly connected to Osogbo. Osun "is extremely popular for her multidimensional fecundities" (Beier 1977: 52). She rules over Osogbo and she is recognized in Nigeria as a state.

In the context of Osogbo that we are discussing, Osun is an historical person. Osun is personified as a Yoruba river that runs through many Yoruba towns. This particular river was not just named after Osun, but the water is her personification and personhood. All Yoruba people take this to be true (Beier 1977: 52). She is the goddess of "the Waters of Life" and spiritual guidance of Osogbo, but her authority extends across Yorubaland (Beier 1977: 52). Osun's mysterious power is preserved in myths, songs, music and histories throughout Yorubaland (Diedre 1995: 115). One important institution that made Osun's fame spread beyond Yorubaland is slavery. Slavery helped spread myths about Osun beyond Yorubaland. So now Osun is known in some parts of the New World slavery and slave-trade (Owomoyela 1971: 123). However, Yoruba worship strongly sustained Osun worship throughout Yorubaland.

So far we have pinpointed some of the religious elements that sustain the awareness of Osun in Osogbo. Osun's myths are impressed in the minds of people. The next chapter will focus on the Osun festival in Osogbo as the most popular annual religious ceremony that brings spiritual leaders, secular leaders and the entire community together annually. There is no way one can talk about Osogbo and Osun without treating the religious value of the Osun festival. Benjamin C. Ray commented on the importance of this subject by saying "the annual Oshun festival at Oshogbo displays Oshun's many powers in a dramatic manner during the sixteen-day celebration" (Ray 2000: 35). Annually, thousands of people participated in the sixteen-day annual celebration of Osun in Osogbo (Ray 2000: 35). As we shall discuss in the next chapter, the festival is an event that attracts various religious leaders, and musicians, in celebration of culture, customs and ritual related to Osun.

Portrait of Osun 53

Selected photos from Osun Grove

54 Portrait of Osun

Portrait of Osun 55

Portrait of Osun 57

3

Celebrating Osun in Osogbo

So far, the focus of the discussion has been on understanding the structure of Osun myths. As pointed out in the previous chapter, Osun controls both the leadership structures and moral standards of the Osogbo people. Osun is so "powerful, indeed empowering" that she attracts people annually to Osogbo for her festival (Diedre 1995: xvi). This chapter turns our attention to how Yoruba people make use of myths annually in reconstructing the Osun festival.

The Osun festival is an annual religious festival in Osogbo, Nigeria. It is a sixteen-day festival that involves the king, chiefs, priests, people of Osogbo and other surrounding villages and cities. It is safe to say that the Osun festival marks the beginning of the calendar year for the people of Osogbo. It is like the way people celebrate the New Near all over the world. Awolalu makes this observation about the Osun festival in Osogbo that many pilgrims attend from different parts of the world (1996: 114).

The Osun festival is a time of ritual, sacrifice, street-processions, dancing, singing, drinking and eating in Osogbo (Omofolabo 1998: 1). It is a period when political and religious leaders remember the inception of Osogbo. At a individual and social level, the festival is a period of honoring Osun with their vows and pledges.

People of Osogbo have a general idea when the festival is to be held in a year but the exact week of the festival is always fixed through Ifa divination. While Osun recognizes and accepts the authority of Ifa oracles (Badejo 1995: 13), it is Orunmila that sets and monitors every aspect of the festival (Badejo 1995: 54).

The Ataoja, who is the king of Osogbo, is the one who is authorized to announce the exact week of the festival at the city centre. One of the reasons for choosing the city centre is to follow the tradition of the early ancestors. Announcing the date is a way of reaffirming his supreme spiritual and political leadership. Ataoja announces the date on a market day, when women and men are carrying out their businesses. The announcement is done in a ceremonial manner and the business women dress up in their best clothes in expectation of the news (Badejo 1995: 139).

The Osun festival usually falls in late August or early September. It has always been around the same period, even before the introduction of the Western calendar in Yorubaland (Centre for African Settlement Studies and Development 1993: 11). August or September is the rainy season in Osogbo and the waters of the Osun River are full to the brim. It is an opportunity to see the power of water and waves in action. One of the beauties of the rainy season in Osogbo is that plants are bushy and forests are thick and dark. This creates a sense of awe and reverence in the minds of the devotees. The rainy season is also a time when plants and wild animals reproduce in great numbers. It is believed that the gods, spirits and ancestors are more actively involved in the Yoruba community at this period than during the other seasons. After the dates have been announced, committed worshippers arrange their annual leave to fall on the dates.

Iya Ewe who is the mother of all children would visit the public markets asking for donations for the festival. As she prays for people from one store to another, people are motivated to give her money for the preparations of the festival. Market places are where everybody meets regularly for business transactions. As soon as the Iya Ewe announces to the people, it is now the responsibilities of those who have heard her to carry the news to their respective homes.

Iwo Popo which means the inspection of the major road is another opportunity for the king and his entourages to notify the entire community about the date of the festival. Before the construction of roads in Osogbo, the only major road that runs through the town has to be cleared by men and women in preparation for the Osun festival. There was no machine then, so everybody has to show up in clearing the bushes in preparation for the day. *Popo* means the main road, and *iwo* means to inspect, that means that the king has to personally inspect the road in a ceremonial way. Drummers and dancers join the King of Osogbo as they all wait for the time of the annual sacrifice.

Ikunle Osun is another preparation that the priests of Osun and their assistants have to do every year. *Ikunle Osun* is the cleaning, dusting and decorating of all Osun images or idols in the shrine of Osun. Priests use special collections of leaves to do the cleaning. By doing this, the people believe that Osun's power would be rejuvenated. Her power would be recharged because *ikunle Osun* involved the use of charms.

A. *Atupa Oloju Merindinlogun* "the Sixteen-Face Lamps"

Following the public announcement of the dates for the Osun festival, an important event occurs: the lighting of the sixteen-face lamps. It is held at night in the courtyard of one of the old palaces in town. This sacred dancing, singing and sacrifice celebration happens four days after the *Iwo Popo*. Many people are present at this spiritual festive meeting. In attendance are the king, queens, hunters, priests of divination, chiefs, boys and girls. One of the special persons in attendance is the *arugba*, who we shall talk more abou in a minute. Each group would dance to the Ifa drums in-turns. One of the popular songs they sing has a line saying *"iya awa di osupa o, Osun le tente"* meaning that "our mother becomes the moon, Osun shines bright." The underlying meaning of this line is that Osun is the light for all her devotees. It indicates that no darkness or wicked spirit would be able to harm them.

Some people are designated to be in charge of the lambs and to make sure they do not quench during the ceremony. These lamps are not ordinary or regular lamps but they are considered spiritual lamps. It is believed these lamps symbolize the welcoming and invitation of the ancestral spirits to the festival. These lamps are symbolically linked to the story that occurred during the inception of Osogbo, when the hunters claimed they heard a voice saying, *Oso Igbo ni mi* translating to "I am the wizard of the forest" (as detailed in chapter two). These leaders further claimed that they fought with seven spiritual beings that Yoruba people call *iwin* "dwarf spirits." *Iwin* (dwarf spirits) are said to be dwarf spirits that roam around at night time especially in the deep jungles. Myths have it that these dwarf spirits are neither good nor bad to people. They only fight back when people tamper with their property, most especially their sleeping mats. The *iwin* are said to be regular residents of *Iroko* trees during the day and wanderers at night. Some hunters, and those who do night shift work, have claimed to see *iwin* "dwarf spirits" at one point or another, though their claims cannot be independently verified.

It was quite understandable when the Osogbo hunters who discovered the Osun grove claimed that they had encountered *iwin* "dwarf spirits" and had seen them holding *atupa olojumerindinlogun* "a sixteen-face lamp" (Centre for African Settlement Studies and Development 1993: 11). With traditional power, the hunters reportedly fought the dwarf spirits, and seized their lamps, which was a good omen for the hunters. It showed that they were men of war who could handle any form of challenges. In defeat, the dwarf spirits left the area for a distant forest. Consequently, the Osun festival begins with the celebration of this victory with spiritual beings over the spirit beings.

During this ceremony, the king and his entourage have to dance round the lamps three times. At the third count, the king and the queens would dance to the shrine of *Ogun* where Timehin, the co-founder of Osogbo, has special shrine for Ogun. Ogun is the god of metals. He coordinates hunting activities and seasons in Yorubaland. Before the king and his people get back to the compound where others were gathered for the celebration of the *atupa olojumerindinlogun,* the priests and the attendants would have parked all the lamps from the scene.

The noise of this ritual can be heard from a far distance. This special annual song and dance contributes to the continuation of Osun myth in Osogbo and in Yorubaland. It creates a sense of awe and reverence in the community (Okpewho, Davies, and Mazrui 1999: 21). Drumming and drums are effective and informational in passing down the Yoruba religion from one generation to another. The music and drums energize the worshippers and encourage them to look forward to the time of the festival.

The other significance of the lighting of *atupa oloju merindilogun* "sixteen-face lamps" is that it provides a rare moment for the king and *Iya Osun* "Osun priestess" to dance in the honor of Osun (Badejo 1995: 110). A female priest had a chance to dance with the king of the land. The queens, Osun priests, babalawo, and hunters join in dancing.

Songs and music for the ritual dance are supplied by a group of hunters who render *ijala* "hunters' dirges" in honor of Osun. This is the night when hunters reenact their forefathers' involvement in the history of Osogbo. These hunters often perform dramatic plays to lighten the spirits of the living and the ancestors. Hunters appreciate the fact that their forefathers risked their lives to gain possession of the land that is today known as Osogbo.

Culturally, *Oju Merindinlogun* "sixteen-face" symbolically represents the sixteen-cowry divination of Ifa oracles (Badejo 1995: 109). A cowry is a small shell that one can collect on the river-bank. Sixteen is the unwritten code of Yoruba divination that the diviners *"babalawo"* combine and interpret for their clients daily. Each pattern of the cowries communicates the mind of Orunmila to the clients. The number sixteen has always been special to Osun. She also knows how to work with sixteen cowries, which is a secret vocational divination. In one of the myths, Osun received her first gift of sixteen cowries called *opele* "cowries" from her husband, Orunmila the father of divination. For her, it was an instrument of the priestly office (Awolalu 1979, 1996). As an intelligent wife who desired not to be left out of her husband's business, Osun learnt the art of manipulating these *opele* "cowries" in divination to get an accurate answer from her husband, Orunmila (Farrow 1996: 42). Osun could beautifully chant *ohun enu ifa* "the Ifa oracles," the scriptural verses of her Ifa divination (Olajubu 1970; Olatunji: 69-86). The quality of her voice often resounds in the ears of the priests and they relate Osun's desires to their customers. To be a diviner, one must know the importance of the sixteen oracles which are annually remembered in the lighting of the lamps.

Number sixteen in the *atupa oloju merindinlogu* is a symbolic number in Yoruba traditional beliefs. As we shall discuss later, the sixteen-face lamps remind the people of the sixteen major *orisa* "divinities" in Yoruba myths (Abimbola 1977). Divinities were said to be the first created beings on earth. They were the emissaries of "Olodumare" God in Yoruba belief.

The second to the last phase of the pre-preparations for the festival is what is called *ijo*. This is a spiritual banquet that the king of Osogbo organizes for all the royal families, chiefs, priests, and their children. It is a time for dining and wining for all the royal members and the priests.

The last pre-preparation for the Osun festival is the *ibo ori ati ibo ade*. This is done a day after the *ijo*. The *ibo ori ati ibo ade* is a combination of two activities. The *ibo ori* is a time when the present king has to offer rituals and sacrifices to Osun and other Yoruba divinities for his personal safety and security throughout the year.

B. The Day of the Festival

On the day of the Osun festival, thousands of devotees, visitors and the media crews gather in Osogbo. This is the final day of a week-long festival. It is the day when people parade in a carnival-like formation from one end of the city to the other (Badejo 1995: 107). Women, men and children, march from the palace of the Ataoja to the Osun grove. They are accompanied by the playing of *sekere* "gourds" *agogo* "bell" jingles and various kinds of drums such as *bembe* to the praise of Osun.

The procession is always long, and for convenience, the line breaks up into sections with different bands playing for them. Dancing and singing, the people would march to the Osun grove. *Onikakaki* "royal trumpeter" would be at the front, leading the procession. Next in line are the *Ayaba* "queens," musicians, chiefs and guards who surround Ataoja (Badejo 1995: 139). As *onikaki* blows his trumpet, the king walks majestically behind him. The nearby residents then troop out to join the entertainment, honor the king and Osun. People whip each other with sticks as an expression of celebration of Osun and their ancestors (Badejo 1995: 145). The audience is entertained by different styles of dance, ranging from slow rhythmic songs to very fast tempo music. Other people, who are not that interested in the festival, stand on their balconies to view the procession.

The king stands out in the procession by his wearing of royal regalia and the chiefs wear their best attires with beads on their necks and arms as symbols of their position. The king is the centre of attraction at the festival. The *emewa* "messengers" of the king carry a very large umbrella to protect the king from sun or rain. A large umbrella is usually a part of the king's wardrobe, and it is specifically designed for his use alone (Badejo 1995: 139).

Like all other Yoruba kings, the Ataoja puts on his *ade* "beaded crown," and one of his messengers carries his *opa ase* "staff of office". In most towns in Yorubaland, whenever a king is invited to a function, and he is unable to attend, he sends one of his *opa ase* "staff of office" with a group of his messengers to represent him. The presence of the staff of office and his representatives signifies that the king is present at the occasion. The staff of office is a very important symbol of power in Yorubaland.

Chiefs, priests, priestesses and the queens surround the king of Osogbo on this special day of the year as he walks majestically past his people. All his chiefs, the guests, men and women adorn themselves with the latest Yoruba traditional dresses. Due to the large number of chiefs in the procession, each one of them wears something unique to distinguish him from the other. The king's face is always partially covered because he wears a beaded crown decorated with strings of beads that cover most parts of his face. However it is a special privilege for anyone to see the king passing by.

1. Activities at the Grove

On Osun day especially, the entering of the grove marks the climax of the events of the Osun festival and it is the best part of the day. People who could not participate in the parade and in the long trek through the city from one end to another would have positioned themselves at the grove waiting for the arrival of the procession. As the Ataoja, Iya Osun, Aworo, Arugba, priests, priestesses and the crowd approach the grove, people who have been waiting there bow in respect to the entourage and to welcome them.

The main Osun shrine is located on the banks of the Osun River. It is a place where the worshippers make invocation, pray and offer sacrifices to Osun. It is a spot where the spiritual leaders of Osogbo talk to Osun on behalf of the citizens. This most sacred spot is where the king offers prayers and sacrifice for the city. The Osun priests and the *babalawo* "ifa priests" would pay their respects to Osun at this spot (Awolalu 1996: 36). They would offer prayer for the peace and prosperity of Osogbo community. This can last for several minutes as the selected chiefs take turns in making specific prayers for the city.

2. The Annual Rituals

At Osun grove, the king pays tribute to Osun and the crowd responds in a loud voice saying *ase* "amen." Others shout *kabiyesi*! "Long live the king!" Some of the invited guests, such as the neighboring *oba* "kings", *baale* "local chairmen", *oloye* "chiefs" and *olori-egbe* "heads of guilds," join the king as he performs the final act of ritual. Ataoja takes time to offer sacrifices to Osun.

As part of the king's final ritual act, he offers a sacrifice to Osun by using the contents of the container that Arugba has been carrying throughout the procession. This is the time to renew "the ancient pact by approaching the river with great ceremony" (Bonnefoy 1991/1993: 146). During the sacrifice, the Ataoja has to stoop low to make a sacrifice to Osun. Seeing him in this posture publicly is a rare gesture expected of a king in Yorubaland. As the political and spiritual authority figure, men are expected to prostrate on the floor for the king to greet him. All female citizens must kneel down to greet the king. For this reason, it is a popular saying in Yorubaland that, *a ki duro ki oba, a ki n bere ki oba*. Nobody ever greet a king in a casual manner. A king is revered and treated as a demi-god by the Yoruba people, and it is an abomination for a king to prostrate himself before any mortal being. If it is done, it is believed that such a person would die within days.

Only in a ritual setting, such as the Osun festival, would one see a king bend so low in public. Osun is honored with such a rare action from the Ataoja once a year. Without such public honor, the Osun festival would not be a complete success. A religious posture of a king prostrating or stooping down before a goddess is a break from traditional practice. It is a significant action and a memorial one in a culture that is dominated by male superiority.

As the king makes this final ritual-sacrifice, the leaders invoke the spirit of Osun to accept the sacrifice as he places it on the river bank (Awolalu 1996: 115). Occasionally, Osun is believed to appear to the crowd in a form of a fish known as *Iko* (Centre for African Settlement Studies and Development 1993: 11). The king literally spreads his hands or palms to welcome the *iko* "fish" into the community. This royal gesture of spreading of hands reminds the large audience of the traditional meaning of the king's official title known as "*Atewogbeja*" meaning "the one who spreads forth his hands to honor the fish." This is in reference to the traditional welcoming of Osun's spirit into the community each year. As can be recalled, the adoption of this official title of Atewogbeja is dated back to the beginning of Osogbo town when Osun appeared to the hunters who first located the place. In response to the king's prayer during the festival, and the gesture of the king, the fish is claimed to have emerged from the water. Its appearance is thought to be an acknowledgement that Osun is pleased with the annual festival and with the people.

3. The King's Annual Address

The final aspect of the Osun festival is the Ataoja's address of the worshippers. His message usually includes the religious issues, political admonishments and appreciation to the audience for attending the festival. In his address, the king outlines the leadership commitments to Osun. He would encourage the citizens to be good and responsible during the year by getting involved in voluntary organizations. The cultural and religious speech is so important that everybody in attendance keeps referring to it for days after the festival. Whatever the king says becomes a point of discussion and action for the leadership of the city and the societal groups in the town. Representatives who attend the festival *jabo* "report" to the members of their groups. Therefore, for the king, the Osun festival is a chance to motivate and challenge the citizens of Osogbo and its environment to cooperate with his leadership (Badejo 1995: 121).

4. Follow-Up Activities

After the spiritual leaders and kings finish their official roles in the festival, the crowd stays behind on the banks of the Osun to collect water in bottles and cans for family members and friends who could not come to the festival. Maude Southwell Wahlman writes "Contemporary Yoruba ritual pots do hold symbolic medicines. Yoruba women who hope to conceive drink fresh water from an *Oshun* pot which also contains riverine pebbles [that] to represent the children of Oshun" (Wahlman 1955: 149). Yoruba believe in the potency of the water. They keep the collected water at home all year round as part of first aid material for the family. As dirty as the water might be, Osun devotees drink and use the water for medicinal purposes (Badejo 1995: 121). It is believed that Osun water can heal them of all their diseases and illnesses. As the worshippers get ready to leave Osogbo, they wash their faces in the river for the last time, believing that the power of Osun will be with them until the next festival.

In summary, the Osun festival provides a yearly opportunity to revisit the historical origins of Osogbo and to educate the young generation of the importance of Yoruba beliefs. The festival provides the opportunity to celebrate Yoruba mythology and cosmology. It offers an opportunity to communicate Yoruba beliefs to the younger generation (Badejo 1995: 53, 63). The Osun festival is therefore a religious, political and cultural event that retains and retells the identity of Yoruba in Osogbo history. The description of the ritual, codified beliefs and superstitious beliefs that surround Osun worship keep the faith alive and free from total corruption.

C. Major Participants in the Annual Festival

Traditional religion and beliefs are part of life for the Yoruba people. Every participant at the Osun festival has to obey the rules governing the divinity and her rituals. This is one of the reasons why one could rely on oral religion to reconstruct the history of a Yoruba goddess, Osun. Benjamin Ray observed that:

> ... in most African societies, there are certain types of religious authorities, such as diviners, prophets, priests, and sacred kings, who perform specific ritual functions. Although these authorities operate in different contexts and in different ways, they serve a common religious purpose: the mediation between man and the sacred (Ray 2000: 103).

For a clear understanding of the Osun festival and its continuation, we need to state the significance of roles that individual religious people play in keeping it alive in Osogbo. Traditionally, people are faithful in playing their roles in the Osun festival. It is believed that if any of the leaders did not play their roles properly, Osun would be very angry with all of them. It is a dangerous thing to fall into the hands of the goddess. Osun is also known as *abijawara* "a veracious fighter". The watchword for every step is caution in fulfilling their religious obligations.

By treating the roles of the following officiating people in Osun festival, we will be able to see how myth is preserved in a religion. These religious leaders that feature every year are the Ataoja of Osogbo, Iya Osun, Aworo Osun and the Babalawo.

1. Ataoja

In continuation with what we have read about the Ataoja as the king of Osogbo, he is also the political head of the Osogbo people. He is considered to be second to all divinities in power, authority and status. He is expected to play his role in making every festival compatible with the historical expectations (DeGraft 1976: 1-25). His roles in the Osun festival are as important as his kingship. As one of the prominent kings in Yorubaland, Ataoja mediates between spiritual beings and his subjects. He seeks for the well being of his people and all the nearby villages and towns and he equally ensures that all the chiefs, business leaders and neighboring kingdoms are fully recognized and acknowledged during the festival where he is the chief host to all invited guests (Awolalu 1996: 110).

2. Iya Osun

Iya Osun, who is the head of men and women in the religious order of Osun, is also the mother figure for all Osun devotees (Osogbo Cultural Heritage Council 1994: 16). She communes daily with Osun in her temple service and regularly acts on her behalf at public functions. She was "involved in the collection of market tolls in the form of food item every day. Such tolls were used for the upkeep of the Osun devotees and as sacrifice to the Osun goddess" (Osogbo Cultural Heritage Council 1994: 16). Is it all about money collection or a means of joining occultism?

As she is called *Iya Osun* "the mother of Osun" literally she has access to many women in the community. The title explains that Iya Osun is in charge of the Osun cult (Badejo 1995: 105). She is presumed to know and understand all things related to Osun more than anybody else in the community. People come from far and near to seek help from Osun through the Iya Osun. As the priestess-in-charge, she has to attend to people who need direct assistance from Osun.

Iya Osun is also the spiritual and official mother of Ataoja, the king of Osogbo (Badejo 1995: 161). The king occasionally seeks the guidance of Iya Osun on certain issues, especially concerning Osun's expectations. All new kings often rely on Iya Osun in fulfilling his role in the Osun festival and rituals. To an average Yoruba person, kings are knowledgeable in everything, but in this case the king relies on a woman's authority, Iya Osun.

Iya Osun's roles are different from that of the *Ayaba*, "queen". The king's relationship with Iya Osun is purely spiritual and there is no need for physical or sexual intimacy between the two, Iya Osun and Ataoja, despite the fact that Yoruba culture encourages the kings and regular men to practice polygamy (Farrow 1996: 51; Schiltz 1985). Spiritual matters are what bring the king and Iya Osun together.

Iya Osun, as the spiritual head of Osun, is the highest priestess in charge of the order. She is present at all meetings for the planning of the festival. The post of Iya Osun is a chieftaincy title that has its origin in Osogbo and is exclusively reserved for a woman who leads in the worship of Osun (Badejo 1995: 161). The Iya Osun is a member of the council of chiefs of which men are in the majority in Osogbo (Osogbo Cultural Heritage Council 1994: 17-18). We have *ilumoyes*, *Ijo Iyalode*, *Ajagunna*, *Akogun, Eesa, Otun Ajagunna, Baale Gbonmi,* and *Balogun.*

In small villages where Osun's influence is not as prominent as it is in Osogbo, *Iya Olorisa* "mother of divinities" presides over all religious affairs that pertain to female divinities, including Osun worship. It has been argued that Iya Osun and Iyalode have economic and spiritual power in their communities (Badejo 1995: 160). In Osogbo, Iya Osun and Iyalode are two different female leaders with different roles in the community. Iyalode is more or less the title for a Yoruba woman who is in charge of commerce and she is the political representative of women of the town while Iya Osun is a female authority figure who is in charge of the Osun shrine.

Iya Osun has a number of men and women who assist her in carrying out her roles in the grove. Among her assistants are Aworo Osun, Balogun Osun and Arugba (Badejo 1995: 161; Bascom 1943: 127). These people have made a covenant with Osun and they work in conjunction with Iya Osun. Collectively, they act as guides for Osun's clients (Beier 1977: 13; Bascom 1943: 127). Iya Osun works with other leaders in planning the Osun festival.

Another role of Iya Osun in the shrine is to prepare the day-to-day sacrifices to Osun. She knows the ingredients required for such sacrifices. Each item on Osun's menu is meaningful to her. On a regular basis, Iya Osun carefully presents the sacrifices and offerings to Osun on behalf of her worshippers. She is also responsible for the welfare of the devotees who visit or reside in Osun grove. She ensures that they all adhere to Osun's standards and expectations while they are in the grove (Badejo 1995: 116).

3. Aworo Osun

Aworo Osun is one of Iya Osun's assistants. Osun is one of few Yoruba female cults where men work under the leadership of women. On behalf of Iya Osun, Aworo makes sure that Arugba perform her duties of carrying the annual sacrifice in a safe environment (Abiodun 2001: 27). Aworo paves the way for the Arugba Osun as she walks among the crowd. He receives instructions from Iya–Osun to take care of Arugba. Aworo's religious role is under the supervision of Iya-Osun (Badejo 1995: 161). For it is a taboo for Arugba to fall during the parade.

At the annual festival people get to know and respect the Aworo Osun.

During the procession, Aworo has a chance to demonstrate to Iya Osun, Arugba, the king, and to Osun that he is capable of doing his job. In addition to this role, Aworo represents the men in the Osun shrine. He regularly assists the Iya Osun in her daily sacrifices. In the grove, he also plays the *dundun,* a kind of drum that makes a special music (Badejo 1995: 118). Songs, drums and dances are parts of the daily ritual during the sacrifices to Osun.

4. Balogun Osun at the Festival

Another prominent character in the Osun festival is the Balogun Osun. Balogun Osun assists Iya Osun. He is a war leader and a protector of Osun's people. He plays both defensive and offensive roles in keeping the grove safe and secure. Balogun in Yorubaland is the commander-in-chief of an entire city. It is a common chieftaincy title and almost all Yoruba communities have one. In Osogbo, the Balogun Osun is a special form of traditional chieftancy which is not common in other Yoruba towns and villages. Balogun Osun is relatively lower in ranks than the Aworo Osun. However the continued existence of this special title and position contributes to the memory of Osun in Osogbo.

5. Babalawo

Individually and collectively, *babalawo* "the Yoruba priests of divination" attend the Osun shrine regularly. During the Osun festival many *babalawo* have to work together to ensure that every item needed for rituals and sacrifices is available in the quality and quantity required for the festival. *Babalawo* understand, devise and discern spiritual matters relating to the arrangements of the Osun festival. The *babalawo* are also known as herbalists because they know how to prevent evil occurrences. Whenever they perceive any problem about Osun's day, they would offer a sacrifice to avert such evil. They know what combination of incantations, leaves, roots, animals, water, soil and ingredients to use in clearing evil spirits from the society.

One of the spiritual weapons of the *babalawo* is incantations. For the Osun festival, they know the exact verses that are relevant to this spiritual occasion. Every rendition of an incantation empowers the priests to discern what the deity expects from the people. Above all, the contents of incantations are mostly from Yoruba myths. Incantations contain and preserve episodes or narratives of the personhood, interactions, and experiences of gods dealing with medical, historical and general issues of people on earth. In Osogbo most incantations have references to Osun. Incantations re-echo mythical history daily and they preserve community history. Regular usage of incantations keeps Osun's faith alive in Osogbo. The residents of Osun grove listen to the stories of Osun on a daily basis. Regularly, babalawo learn about the personhood of Osun. Incantations preserve the records of how gods and Yoruba ancestors worked together in their history. The *babalawo* in their oracles always encourage and practice repetition of the verses in incantations. Some verses are said to be so efficacious that when they are repeated three, seven, or twelve times in the morning, afternoon and evening they can solve problems (Bascom 1943: 128). Incantations work for those who strictly follow the directions of the priests to the letter. Incantations are beautiful oral poetries that sound well and, at the same time, are full of spiritual messages and traditional wisdom.

The *babalawo* who is deeply involved in the planning and execution of the plans of the Osun festival is usually one of the leading figures among the priests and he would have been a regular consultant for Osun leaders during the year. His involvement in the planning guarantees the continuation of relationships between Osun and Orunmila in the Yoruba tradition. It reminds the community that Orunmila at one time was married to Osun. It is also evidence that Orunmila and Osun shared some things in common, as divinities, sojourners and diviners during their earthy existence.

To ensure the smooth running of the Osun festival, this particular Babalawo would work closely with Ataoja and Iya Osun. From the beginning of the planning to the end of it, the king would continuously summon the *babalawo* and Iya Osun to his palace for meetings and deliberations. One of the roles of the *babalawo* is to foretell the weather condition of the chosen dates and to make rituals that would guarantee an accident-free festival. He would prescribe the ritual ingredients for such sacrifices as may be needed. He would also warn the leaders of any imminent dangers and guide them in taking the necessary precautions. Ifa oracles are known to be *arinu-rode olumoran okan* "the one who knows the inner thoughts of all the people" (Farrow 1996: 42). He speaks to the people as he receives the revelations and directions from heavens.

The involvement of *Babalawo* "priests" in the Osun festival speaks for the way her influence has been aided by *babalawo* traditional practices around the world. Historically, Osun was familiar with the act of divination too (Badejo 1995: 2). The Yoruba people believe that originally the sixteen cowries of divination were the property of Osun. She learned the skill of reading these sixteen cowries from Orunmila (Badejo 1995: 92). In Yorubaland none of the sixteen divinities is widely known as having the skill and knowledge of Ifa-divination apart from Osun and Orunmila. The idea of Osun having the knowledge and skills of divination is not widely known in Yorubaland (Badejo 1995: 93). But her involvement with divination balances the male-female issue among the Yoruba divinities. Not only do Osun praise-poems testify to her gender recognition amidst the socio-cultural hierarchy, but her annual festival sustains her divinity in Osogbo (Badejo 1995: 9, 14).

6. Arugba

In Osun worship, Arugba is the virgin lady chosen to carry the Osun sacrifice on her head across Osogbo town on the final day of the Osun festival (Abiodun 2001: 27). Arugba is the youngest among the leadership in Osun festival. She is chosen from the ruling royal family's girls. She is a virgin princess. The process of appointing Arugba can be very challenging.

The Yoruba people have ways of discerning if a girl or a boy is sexually active. One way is by asking the young children if they have been involved in such acts. It is dangerous to lie to an adult in the Yoruba kingdom. The children know that the spirits of the ancestors are watching and listening to every conversation. One has no choice but to tell the truth. The second way of verifying information is by asking other children and their parents. Every member of the community knows the importance of telling the truth. The third way of determining the truth is to ask the *babalawo* "priests of divination". As we have mentioned earlier, the priests can tell about anybody's past, present and future by consulting the Ifa oracles. The priests can reveal the past sexual life of the Arugba candidates to the selected.

Once the Arugba has been chosen, she carries the sacrifices every year until she is ready for marriage. The Arugba is not permitted to be sexually active while she still holds the position. When she decides to marry, another person is selected to take-up the responsibilities. Anyone who marries a former Arugba is expected to worship Osun as their family goddess (Beier 1977: 16).

On the final day of the festival, the Arugba carries the annual sacrifice in a calabash, which is made out of a gourd, across the city with the entourage around her. Months before the festival, the Arugba will have made Osun grove her home in order to be filled with the spirit of

Osun (Badejo 1995: 162). During this time, she has less contact with the outside world. The two men that she sees regularly at the grove are the Aworo Osun and Balogun Osun. By adopting this secluded lifestyle, the temptation of living a promiscuous life is reduced to a minimum and the men that she relates with know that they cannot have sex with the Arugba. While the Arugba attends school during the academic year, she lives in the Osun grove. At school, her colleagues respect her for being a virtuous spiritual girl who will represent the city. Her male friends dare not ask her for a date or to make any sexual advances towards her for fear that she is *omo orisa* "a child of divinity." The Arugba is accorded a similar level of respect as that given to Osun. Fear is built in the minds of these children about the powers of Osun from their early years. As a student, she represents her age group as Osun welcomes both young and old to her festival.

One of the rules guiding the girl is that she is not permitted to carry any load on her head during her appointment as Arugba. Carrying goods on one's head is a common practice in Yorubaland and it is one of the easiest ways of moving things from one place to another. The market women, the farmers, the children and everybody who lives in Osogbo are used to carrying loads on their heads from one place to another (Badejo 1995: 162). The only thing that the Arugba is required to carry on her head is the *ebo* "sacrifice" of the annual festival.

On the festival day, as the Arugba carries Osun's sacrifice from the city to the river she is believed to be totally possessed by the spirit of Osun. At that moment, she operates under the influence of the spirit. She is in a state of ecstasy (Omofolabo 1998: 38). The Arugba intensely concentrates on her steps because she must not fall and the sacrifice on her head must not tip off. The atmosphere she carries the sacrifice within is so noisy and crowded that she needs all the assistance she can get in performing her service successfully. Aworo and others who understand the significance of her task surround her during the procession as she walks through the crowd (Badejo 1995: 133). Her spiritual achievement is fulfilled for the year when she successfully brings the sacrifice to the Osun grove.

7. Crowds

A major criterion for measuring the success of the Osun festival is the number of participants. The second way is to see that the event is free of accidents. Constantly, prayers are offered for the safe arrival of participants in the festival and also for the safe return of the participants to their respective homes. All the leaders work in harmony to make sure the festival is accident free.

Osogbo hosts a large crowd during the week of the Osun festival. People come to Osogbo from all the neighboring villages, towns and cities just for the celebration. Most citizens of Osogbo who live in other parts of the Yoruba states and other countries come to witness the annual ritual. Among the crowds at the festival are the entertainers, artisans, youth groups, representatives from other Yoruba communities, and associations of petty traders. These groups of people form the large part of the crowd that makes the festival the historical and religious event of the year (Badejo 1995: 117). Each of these participants arrives in Osogbo each year with a determination to be blessed by the spirits.

Women and men come to renew their vows with Osun. Like the kings, local chairmen, chiefs and heads of the guilds in the area, men and women take monetary gifts to the king and offer sacrifices to Osun. Barren women who were cured come to Osun priests with gifts of appreciation. These women attend the festival with the purpose of offering sacrifice and prayer for their family members.

Those who can afford to pay for transportation and accommodation take their children to the festival to secure protection against any spiritual attacks and to meet with other children. The children of Osun "*Omo Osun*" are quite visible during the parade and at the shrines. Sometimes, they wear uniforms known as *aso egbe*. It is a sign of the spiritual bond that exists and binds these children together (Badejo 1995: 143). The festival day is called *ojo odun* "day of festivity".

After the parade, when the king has made the final sacrifice and read his speech, some of the children immerse themselves in the Osun River while the grown-ups assist them in bathing in it. Kate Miriam Loewenthal and Marco Cinnirella argued that such bathing in a sacred river fosters a strong self-esteem in individual worshipper and in developing social relationship within a religious group (Loewenthal and Marco 2003: 126).

D. Other Important Places and Things associated with the Osun

Here are some relevant places and things that participants always remember about the Osun festival.

1. The Osun Grove

The Osun grove is the land near the Osun River. It is a common practice in Yorubaland to designate a landed property for some divinity in each city and village.

On the day of the festival, very early in the morning some people position themselves at the grove. One reason for this is to find a better position to view the last part of the festival and the second reason is to enjoy the serenity of the grove before the arrival of the noisy crowd. A family of four or more members could lose one of its people among the crowd, so it is better to wait at the final spot of the procession at the grove.

During the year, Osun grove is out of bounds to the farmers and hunters, whose means of livelihood are related to it. The grove has been preserved for a long time hence the acres of land have become thick dark forest and left uncultivated for years. It is a typical tropical forest of Osogbo. These features create special effects that raise the sense of awe and reverence for divinities. People believe the grove is spiritually charged, and it is the home of the divinities and evil spirits. Creeping things and beasts freely live on the sacred piece of land. Although the Yoruba depend on hunting for wild meat, in Osun grove it is forbidden. The Osun grove, therefore, is a safe haven for birds, animals and fish that want to escape the hunters.

As mentioned earlier, the grove provided a security for Osogbo during the previous inter–tribal warfare as it made it difficult for the invaders to gain access to the Osogbo. Some people credited Osun for providing such safety and protection for the city while others thought that it was the natural protective demarcation of the city. Together the forest and the river made access to Osogbo very difficult for its enemies. The Fulani Jihadists learned their lesson the hard way (Ajayi and Smith 1964: 34). These Islamic extremists could not find their way out of the jungle of Osogbo and many of them died on the outskirts of the city. Those who survived left in frustration (Badejo 1995: 115).

In this century, though Yoruba people still migrate to other Yoruba cities they leave room for spirituality (Beier 1977: 15). Almost all Yoruba cities and villages have *igbo orisa* "divinities forest." In different villages and towns, such sacred land may be called *Igbo Oro* "Oro forest," *Igbo igbale* "Igbale forest," or other names after the prevailing cult or deity of the town. The sacredness and serenity often scare property developers from building houses on the land.

Osun grove is a symbolic pilgrim center. It is a sacred forest that reminds the Yoruba people of the importance of gods and goddesses in Osogbo. It is a Mecca of Osun. The Osun grove is a testimonial for the children and people in Osogbo. Kare Tate gives a genuine warning to potential tourists to be careful in wherever they go in Osogbo.

> It should be noted, tourists are usually only allowed in the anterooms of shrines. This is viewed as important to protect both the shrine from spiritual defilement, (as well as tourists from taboos), and the powerful forces that might unsettle the uninitiated. Pilgrims are reminded this is a sacred precinct and proper respect is required around the shrines, river, and sacred forest (Tate 2006: 108).

Sacred places are spiritually charged. They are different from mere tourist centers. Other forms of Yoruba divinities that often use reserved sacred forests are the *Egungun* "masquerades" and *Oro* "secret cults." Their worship always required the preservation of landed properties called *Igbo Egun* or *Igbo Oro*. During their festivals these religious cults end their celebration at their sacred forests too. *Egungun* "masquerades", are known to be the worship of the spirits of the dead. During their festival they emerge from *igbale* "a secret portion of the *igbo Egungun*" a sacred land allocated to them. They wear elaborate costumes, carved masks, carved statues, and well decorated religious paraphernalia to disguise themselves from people (Onyewuenyi 1984: 242). Some people wonder how a normal person could hide behind such heavy masks for hours without magical powers (Bascom 1973: 89). *Ojubo orisa* "shrines" and *odo Osun* "Osun river" are in close proximity to the Osun forest in order to reinforce people's idea during the Osun festival (Awolalu 1996: 144).

The Osun festival gives the people an opportunity to get closer to Osun grove. The *igbo Osun* "the forest of Osun" raises the spiritual beliefs of the city (Badejo 1995: xvi). In addition to its spiritual advantages, the worshippers have a chance to listen to the sounds of birds, feel the cool breeze and see the beauty of the natural habitat of Yorubaland. The smell of the forest could be equated to the aroma of burning incense in temples and synagogues. In the grove, there are "trees higher than the medieval cathedrals which hide their powerful bodies" from the public eyes (Beier 1977: 19). It is rare to see a forest designated for a goddess in other Yoruba towns and villages but Osun has a grove in Osogbo that preserves her memory.

The Osun grove is a perfect setting to end the festival because of its natural beauty, cool atmosphere and presence of shaded trees for the crowds. The Osun festival is conducted during the rainy season because it is the time "when the power, beauty, and potentials of Osun River are most evident" to the people (Badejo 1995: 115). The waves of the river are powerful and the currents are high, so people get a rare opportunity to admire the power of the river.

Another point that makes the grove a factor of continuation of Osun worship was the role it played during the nineteenth century inter-tribal and religious wars in Osogbo. People can still recollect the stories of how the Moslem Fulani from the North invaded some Yoruba cities, especially the Oyo Empire (Badejo 1995: 158; Ajayi and Smith 1964: 33). When the Jihadists got to Osogbo, the Osun grove formed a natural barrier against their horses. The Fulani Jihadists had no understanding of the tropical region and hence could not conquer the city (Beier 1977: 24). Osogbo is situated at a geographical boundary where the savannah land turns into a thick, dark tropical forest. This change in terrain made it difficult for the Fulani horses to be effective in hunting down the residents of Osogbo. Tsetse flies, the dangerous bugs of the south, which cause a condition known as sleeping sickness, killed many of the Fulani horses, and the diseases spread throughout their military camps. All these factors gave Yoruba in Osogbo victory over the Fulani. These stories are recounted at the Osun festival yearly (Law 1977).

Unfortunately, the Osun grove is now being encroached by the Nigerian government and the traditional government. At one time, the king rented out part of the Osun forests for agricultural research. Unexpectedly, this deal failed to materialize, and some people attributed this failure to unhappiness with the proposal. It is pointed out that "the battle against destruction of trees, sacred animals and fish in the sacred river, still goes on because of the varieties of animals that reside in and around the groves" (Beier 1977: 18). Requests for permission to use the Osun grove for one purpose or the other are being received. For instance, the Antiquities Department of the Federal Government of Nigeria is involved in preserving the grove as a natural habitat for humanity and animals, but to the majority of Yoruba people, the Osun grove is a supernatural habitat for the divinities. In African religion, spiritual forces are believed to reside in rivers, lakes, lagoons, oceans, under the *iroko* tree and at road intersections (Beier 1977: 52). Yoruba people make sacrifices and perform their rituals mostly at the above mentioned places (Ray 2000: 78). Under the direction of the herbalists, Yoruba people believe that gods and goddesses *gba ebo* "accept the sacrifice" from them. Such beliefs and practices are the elements that contributed to the continuation of Osun worship in Yorubaland.

2. Images and Sculptures in the Osun Grove

There are lots of statues and carvings in the grove. In preparation for the sacrifices, the statues in the grove are decorated with palm-fronds weeks before the festival. The Osun grove is a ritual arena of Osun. As far as the Osogbo people are concerned, the Osun grove is holy ground. It houses not only the Osun shrines, but also shrines for other Yoruba divinities who are close associates of Osun (Beier 1977: 17). The relationship that Osun has with other Yoruba divinities, during the festival and throughout the year has contributed to the continuation of

Osun worship in Yorubaland.

In addition to images of Osun in the grove, there are images of other divinities too. Some of the images or idols are beautifully designed, while others are scary and terrible works of art which do not represent the pictures of gods or the works of art in the Yoruba community (Onyewuenyi 1984: 242), as these images were made a long time ago, to mirror the essence of "gods and goddesses" being with us (Beier 1977: 7). They were made by the ancestors and they were given similar honors of the ancestors. These images stand as testimonials that the Yoruba believed in gods before the arrival of Christian and Islamic missionaries. Such sacred places are for spiritual retreat, meditation and the performing of rituals. People who attend the annual festival often go home with the impression that Yoruba divinities cooperate among themselves for the welfare of their people.

Each image communicates a divine message to people. The local artists who carved and molded the Osun sculptures depersonalized their work to create a sense of awe for the divinities (Beier 1962: 26). In their creation, they were not intending to make an exact representation of Osun, or of other divinities, but were willing to create a figure that would stimulate people in worship and at festivals. They are not intended to be admired, but to scare the people and to create an unforgettable impression. Yoruba believe that *ti omode o ba de ibi eru, yio ma se ako* "if a child does not enter into a scary place, terrified place, there is a tendency for him or her to be boastful and proud."

Figures of a religious deity for worship are not only scary-looking but often these images are charmed and soaked in voodoo power. The uninitiated cannot touch the idols or any of the ritual objects in the shrine. It is only by spiritual guidance or supervision that one may touch any of them. There are some Yoruba idols that the uninitiated are not allowed to see. Under no circumstances would anybody dare to toy with these religious images. Yoruba religious idols or images are not ordinary souvenirs to feel, to touch, or to purchase at gift shops. They are not created for making money or to be used as toys. Each idol is made for a reason, "the need of the community determines the artist's production. His art is never "art for art's sake" (Onyewuenyi 1984: 243).

Many of the images in the Osun grove are rusted and they are not that impressive to the eyes. Without the religious significance, these images could not have attracted tourists to the Osun grove. However, Osun worshippers are not concerned with the beauty of the images but perceive them as religious icons with electric spiritual power. People rarely touch them for fear that they may be spiritually possessed.

The religious images in the Osun grove add to the sanctity of the grove and the festival. Just before the annual festival begins, these disfigured, rusted, and dilapidated images are painted and decorated with fresh palm-fronds just for the festival period (Badejo 1995: 118).

3. The Shrines of Other Yoruba Gods in the Grove

In the Osun grove, there are various shrines to other Yoruba deities (Awolalu 1996: 114). At the grove, during the final hours of the Osun festival, many participants gather in front of their specific family shrines for prayer (Badejo 1995: 119). The Yoruba believe divinities are more active and attentive when worshipped at shrines than in homes (Beier 1977: 52). Moving from one shrine to another is an opportunity to tap into various sorts of spiritual powers on the same day.

For Osun to allow other divinities to be worshipped in her grove is a testimony that Osun is very accommodating in promoting peaceful co-existence with other divinities (Badejo 1995: 2). It is noted that "oral literature confirms that Olodumare, the Supreme Being, gave Osun her powers" to share responsibilities and authority with her colleagues

(Badejo 1995: xvi). Divinities living in the same grove foster interpersonal relationships among the devotees. The Osun festival is a time of informing, educating, and promoting cultural and religious peaceful co-existence in Osogbo. This sixteen-day event is structured in such a way that individuals have a chance to renew their allegiance to their family gods and collectively enjoy the sacred presence of Osun.

Yoruba people do not have regular contact and communication with the Almighty God. But such activity as the Osun festival provides a moment of reflection on the creation and creatures for the worshippers. There are differences between the gods and the Almighty God. God does not have a designated shrine in Yorubaland. Shrines are for the lesser gods and spirits of the dead. The Yoruba people recognize *Olorun Olodumare* as God, and His supreme ancestor is *Oduduwa* (Adeoye 1979: 1-5).

From the beginning to the end of the Osun festival, the Yoruba people pray to God through her. Osun is praised and adored, so that she may secure protection and provision for them throughout the year (Abimbola 1994: 75-76). Although Yoruba give credits to gods for safety and satisfaction, the gods depend on the supernatural provisions of *Olorun Olodumare* whose worship requires no liturgy, iconography, or official priesthood. God in Yoruba thought is an example of an abstract divinity too mighty to be captured by any artistic, literary, or idealistic simplification but he is involved in human affairs.

Other members of Orisa Yoruba (gods of Yoruba) are the *egungun* "masquerades", *Oro, Obatala/Orisa-nla, Orunmila/ Ifa, Sango, Oya, Iyemoja, Osun Osogbo, Esulalu, Orisa oko, Sonpona, orisa ibeji* and *Osanyin*. All of the above mentioned divinities owe their being and existence to *Olorun Olodumare* "God Almighty." It is accepted that God can command them to act on his behalf in the Yoruba kingdom. Human beings are always on the receiving end of the gods' actions on earth (Badejo 1995: xx).

4. Other Yoruba Religious Beliefs that Feature in the Osun Festival

There are other related daily practices that help the Osogbo people in reconstructing the history of Osun festival. *Owe* (proverbs), *itan* (stories), *alo* (riddles and jokes) and *asa-ibile* (cultural practices) and other related literary forms are conceptual frameworks upon which most of the annual festival is based. The Osun festival is based on common beliefs, thoughts and practices with which most people are familiar.

i. Oriki, Poem and Poetry: Osogbo people give praise to Osun daily in forms of greetings. The praise poems are called *oriki*, and every Yoruba person and family has got at least one. The elders, men, women, wives, drummers and friends often use the *oriki* to praise one when one is in a good or bad mood. In rural areas, people use *oriki* every morning in exchange of greetings. So during the festival, the participants exchange greetings using the *oriki* of Osun. Whenever time permits them, men, women and children sing songs of Osun in choruses as part of the regular greetings.

During birth ceremonies, weddings, burials, or house warming parties, drummers and musicians may put the *oriki* Osun into poems that guests may dance to. The drummers can use *bata* or *gangan* drums to make such music for hours. Occasionally, especially during burial ceremonies, the drummers often use Osun praises to entertain the crowds and to remind them of the significance of Osun (Badejo 1995: 2). Such regular repetitions contribute to the historical significance of Osun in Osogbo. This is summarized by one author as follows,

> Repetition embellishes the literary style employed here. The poem is intoned in three phases, the first of which introduces Osun to the listeners by a series of references to the townships where she is worshipped, townships through which the Osun River flows, and townships which have other historical connections to Osun Osogbo (Badejo 1995: 3).

This practice forms part of the social life of the Yoruba people and their culture.

Akosori "poems" are another way of retaining Yoruba culture in the memory. The best source of hearing the correct form of Yoruba poem is through the Ifa priests, such as Yemi Eleburuibon (Diedre 1995: xx). The *akosori* "praise" is one of the Yoruba's best ways of retelling the past activities of divinities and ancestors for the current community (Diedre 1995: xvi). Drummers, priests, chiefs and elders also recite the *akosori* to the community to remind them of their past. Most of the Yoruba incantations are in the form of *akosori* (Beier 1977: 13). The clients are encouraged to render it from memory. For example in one Yoruba poem, Osun is praised as "*Osun Seegesi Olooya-iyun*, which means Osun, the owner of the flawless, perfectly carved beaded comb" (Diedre 1995: 2). This praise tells us about how neatly Osun uses make-up on her face and appearance, but one does not have to read this character from religious scripture (Abiodun 2001: 27). Yoruba are skilled in remembering such powerful descriptions and the use of words in any given context.

ii. Prayer, Petition and Vow: One of the uses of *oriki* is a means of *mu ori* Osun *wu* "winning the heart of Osun" but the more important usage of Oriki is being part of Yoruba prayers (Diedre 1995: 13). During the festival, women and men gather to present their cases and needs to Osun in the form of *oriki* (praises). Osun as one of the goddesses who care for the needs of men and women responds to their petitions. People face the direction of the Osun River in prayer, believing that Osun will respond better during the festival (Beier 1977: 7, 20).

Another important act of praise in prayer is shown in the way people redeem their vows. Some of the people merely attend the festival to fulfill their vows. In difficult times, the majority of the Yoruba people make vows that remain binding on them until they are fulfilled. At the Osun festival, people keep their vows, pledges, promises, or covenants by paying in cash and in kind. Believers, who had been childless for many years, come to the annual festival with high expectations that Osun will assist in their childbearing. So on receiving answers to their prayers, they return to thank Osun by offering sacrifices to her (Diedre 1995: 84). By redeeming their vows, they hope they can get more miracles from her. A Yoruba proverb says *ti omode ba dupe ana, yio ri omiran gba* meaning "if a child is grateful for a favor received yesterday from an adult, that child will receive more favor in the future."

As people gather in Osogbo for the festival, they seize the opportunity to consult local priests for spiritual medicines. Osun water alone cannot cure all kinds of diseases and illness. The Yoruba believe that you need the power of words called *ofo* "incantations" to experience supernatural healing and deliverance from all sorts of diseases. *Babalawo* "priests of divination" are the people who specialize in recommending the right *ofo* "incantations" for various ailments. They know how to conjure Osun's spirit through Ifa to cure, heal, or deliver people from their individual or family problems. The Yoruba have the attitudes of calling the gods through incantations more frequently and hardly debate or doubt the divine intervention (Beier 1977: 13).

In addition to the power of using the right words to communicate with the ancestors and divinities, the Yoruba believe that one has to frequently combine the power of leaves, roots and plants to procure healing and protection from all kinds of diseases. For this reason, people who attend the Osun festival collect Osun water, and consult the priests for charms that can only be found easily in the Osogbo area. In the Yoruba religion, shrines, sacred forests, road intersections, and *eti odo* "river banks" are sacred places to offer sacrifices and rituals. The priests can prescribe that people offer sacrifice to divinities very early in the morning before one talks to anybody, or during the mid-day, sometimes around 1pm, or 12 midnight. It is believed that these are times when the spirits of divinities are more active in Yorubaland. Observations of these rules contribute to the effectiveness of prescribed medication or charms, and it creates awe in people.

iii. Singing, Dancing, and Costume Dressings: During the festival, the sweet sound, and high pitch of singers fills the air daily. Music and songs form the integral part of the whole sixteen-day celebration (Diedre 1995: 4). Most of the Osun devotees enjoy the fun more than the actual ritual. It is full of emotional expressions, images and dances. Yoruba people celebrate the Osun festival with great performing arts, crafts, music and dance. It is a time for the elaborate display of Yoruba culture. People's spirits, minds and bodies gain satisfaction in music (Diedre 1995: xvi).

Group dancing and colorful uniform dressing make the Osun festival memorable. Adults and children wear colorful clothing to express their desire for the year. Kings, chiefs, priests, queens, princes and princesses alike wear their best native dress on the day. In Yoruba myths, Osun specialized in the production of tie-dyed dresses and people must honor her with best outfits (Diedre 1995: 2, 165). We should not forget Osun's first encounter with the early settlers when they accidentally broke her pots of tie-dye, Osun wept and cried aloud that all her pots had been shattered because she loved textiles. During the festival, her devotees proudly wear locally made tie-dye uniforms to honor Osun.

The Yoruba people dress in different colors as the occasion may demand (Diedre 1995: 165). The participants in the Osun festival wear gold, yellow and white dresses (Diedre 1995: 108). These are bright colors, dull colors are meant for the worship of *Esu*, a devil to the Yoruba. People in particular professional and religious groups usually wear colorful uniforms to identify themselves in the crowd (Brincard

1985: 25). The dancers, singers and drummers dress in the same style to differentiate themselves from other invited groups that are part of the crowd. Singing praises such as: "OMO OWA OLUYEYE, OMO OBOKUN – the child of Owa, the child of Obokun. OMO ODO KAN, ODO KAN TI WON NPE L'OSUN – the child of one one river known as Osun. OMO ATENIGBOLA OLODO IDE – the child who is highly honour, the owner of the precious gold" (Osogbo Cultural Heritage Council 1994: 53).

Kings, chiefs, priests, priestesses and politicians wear the most expensive materials and different sizes of beads to differentiate themselves from the crowds. Beads and heavy fabrics are symbols of wealth and honor in the Yoruba community (Brincard 1985: 27). A Yoruba proverb says *irini si, ni isoni lojo* meaning one's appearance or dressing would earn one honor or otherwise.

iv. Drums and Musical Instruments: Wherever and whenever Yoruba people hear drums and religious songs, they get so excited and emotional. Drums form part of the Osun culture and festival. The most popular drums that people dance to during the Osun festival are the *bembe*. There is historical significance in the use of *bembe* drum during the Osun festival. *Bembe is a* "side-drum" musical instrument that is commonly used by the Ijesha people of Yorubaland (Herskovits 1966: 218). The early immigrants brought this culture with them to Osogbo during the resettlements. *Bembe*, since then, has become the official drums of the Osun festival (Olugunna 1959: 25). It is a historical reminder of Osun and Osogbo's historical union.

Ayan is the person who plays drums in Yorubaland. There is no evidence of a drum called *ayan* as indicated by Deidre (Diedre 1995: 54). Another name for a drummer is *onilu*. Individuals who play specific drums could be called by the names of their drum sets. For example, those who play *bembe* are called *"onibembe,"* those play *gangan* are called *onigangan*, those who play *"omele"* drums are called *"olomele"* and those who play *"bata"* are called *"onibata"*. In any case, the *bembe* drum reminds people of Osun in the Yoruba community. It is her favorite drum. The use of drums stimulates spirit possession. Drummers may control the crowd to stop, stand, to turn right or left through drums. The leading drummers may suggest another song or the change of beats through its sound.

In a creative way, the drummers may come up with different kinds of songs during the festival. Occasionally, they form controversial songs that may arouse the people's feeling. In 1982, there was religious "tension between the traditionists and the Muslims over the Osun Festival" (Diedre 1995: 164). The tension was captured in one song the following year that ridiculed Muslim men for wearing their turbans (Diedre 1995: 164). Osun songs became campaign slogans against the people who had converted to Islam (Peel 1967: 292-306).

Drumming and musical instruments stimulate spirit possession (Diedre 1995: 54). Yoruba music is often deafeningly loud. People claim to hear the voices of the spirits when they are in a state of ecstasy, jerking, falling down, and staggering in different directions. This remarkable sight often lingers in the memories of the attendees for years. Such scenes are not common in day-by-day religious worship (Beier 1977: 17).

E. Summary of the Osun Festival

In summary, the Osun festival is a sixteen-day celebration of Osun, the origin of Osogbo, the independence of Osogbo, and victory of the Osogbo people over human and natural challenges. It is a celebration of Yoruba culture, arts, and divinities. It is a remembrance of the significance of the Osun River. The Osun River became the best water resource for the early settlers and it forms a natural defence against religious warriors. Osun's annual festival is a remembrance of how the early settlers journeyed to the new settlement and how they struck deals with Osun, the goddess of the river. Today the river has become a source of healing for the afflicted in Osogbo and beyond, while the festival has also become a forum where people and political leaders meet the kings, chiefs, priests, priestesses and Osogbo people to promote their agenda. It is a time when the people celebrate the divine assistance of Osun and appreciate the generational wisdom of the elders and ancestors (Diedre 1995: 140). It is a religious and cultural festival that celebrates the communion of the living and the dead.

To some Christians, Muslims and liberal minds, the Osun festival is idol worship. Not all residents of Osogbo believe the popular claims of the king and the devotees of Osun. Those people think of Osun as one of those fabricated mythological figures that the forefathers manufactured to create fear in the minds of innocent people. For example, some Christians and Muslims consider the Osun festival as a celebration of the evil spirits and demons. Those who participate and believe in Osun are going to hell after death. To discourage the following of demonic spirits and the deceit of Yoruba leaders, some evangelical Christian churches hold services in their churches and at homes on the week of the festival to "bind" all the spirits and the influence of Osun from Osogbo. To them, the Osun festival is considered to be a satanic influence on people who need godly deliverance.

In addition to the voices of such critics in Osogbo there are some who just go to the festival to make money. It is a time when petty traders, either believers or not, come to market their products. Big business corporations such as the manufacturers of soft drinks make a lot of money during the festival. Hotels are booked to capacity. All small businesses have huge turnovers during the festival.

Osun sees everybody as part of her city. People of different religions, ages, genders and nationalities are welcome to the festival. As an inclusive faith, Osun worship does not discriminate against any human being or divinity. One author said that Osun championed the concept of "balanced and equitable co-existence between men and women" (Diedre 1995: xxiv). The Osun is subservient to no male authority; neither does she harbor any hatred towards any tribe or people. In worshiping her, both men and women jointly honor her in Yoruba traditional religion (Diedre 1995: xvi). The Osun festival provides an opportunity for everybody to publicly come together in her celebration (Diedre 1995: 54).

This chapter concludes the first main part of our discussion on the roles of myths in the history of Osun worship in Yorubaland. We cannot necessarily cover all the Yoruba beliefs that feature annually in the Osun festival, but so far we have pointed out the historical roles of the king, the Iya Osun, Arugba, Aworo, Osun grove, the crowds and other divinities in Osun festival. We have outlined different ways they contribute to the continuation of Osun worship in Yorubaland. The next part of this book will focus on the use of myths in the history of the Yoruba religion outside the Yorubaland.

4

Osun in the New World

This chapter opens the second part of this book, which is the treatment of a Yoruba goddess, Osun, in the New World. In the first part, we briefly summarized different methods relating to the study of Yoruba religion in the Old and the New Worlds. We also described the Osun worship in Osogbo, the headquarters of her shrine. In this second part we shall study the myths of Osun in Cuba, Brazil, Jamaica, Trinidad and Haiti. Scholars have the unexamined assumption that *orisa* is from the Yorubaland, therefore, they mentioned the connection of the tradition in passing. The assumption, even though not false, does not carry the force of self-validating truth. We will argue that the influence of an African religion Osun Osogbo, has grown beyond its original continent through the survival of Yoruba myths in the New World. Kola Abimbola writes "Today, Orisa tradition and culture is practiced by about 100 million people in Argentina, Australia, Benin Republic, Cuba, France, Germany, Ghana, Haiti, Italy, Jamaica, Japan, Mexico, Sierra Leone, Spain, Togo, Trinidad and Tobago, UK, USA, Venezuela, etc." (Abimbola 2006: 1). Orisa, and particularly Osun, is practiced in different parts of the world. We, therefore, have to focus on a few countries to describe the significance of myths in sustaining a religious worship.

The present task is to study the mythological symbols that sustain Osun worship in the New World. Douglas Allen in the *Myth and Religion in Mircea Eliade* is of the opinion that symbols play major roles in influencing people's lifestyle and belief around the world. He said, "Religious symbols are put together in narrative form so that these true stories reveal a sacred history of events that took place in sacred time and provide exemplary models for allowing mythic beings to make sense of their model of being in the world" (Allen 2002: 188). Here is a poem that contains certain symbols of Osun:

> Oshun, sweet River Goddess
> For Orisha Oshun
> Oshun
> Lovely River Goddess
> your bosom green,
> Swells with abundance
> We drink from the fountain
> of your waters,
> it is sweet as the honey
> you desire.
> Heavy river scent
> brought on the rain
> is heady and intoxicating,
> a perfume
> that is tied to breadth
> of the soul.
> Beautiful Oshun,
> gracious River Goddess,
> granting petitions
> to those who know her mystery
> Fertile, rich
> enchanting seductress... (Stevenson 2001: 66)

In this poem, we have the symbols of the sweet; River, bosom, green, fountain, waters, honey, scent, rain, intoxication, perfume, breadth, soul, beauty, gracious, petitions, fertility, richness and seduction in just a poem. These symbols made powerful and unforgettable images in the mind of the Yoruba community. No wonder the people still recollect Osun in the New World.

Osun, a Yoruba goddess, represents one of hundreds of divinities that had her origin in Africa. It is now becoming impossible to call such a group of religious activity African religion. For lack of a better term, we can call them the African originated, African cultured, or African saturated religion. These suggested lists have their problems. The term 'Africa' is too broad for a reference to a religion that comes from a corner of a continent.

The description of Yoruba myths in the New World needs to be connected to a specific group and town in Nigeria (Platvoet 1996: 55). The new trend in African religious studies is to avoid the error of generalization. The use of the term "Africa" is too broad a term. On the other hand people should not work on the microscopic aspect of the community without making a reference to what is happening in the world religions. It has been pointed out that, "in the history of the study of African traditional religions, the African studies have moved from amateur ethnography towards academic anthropology through contributions by liberal Christian missionaries and more recently the historical studies" (Platvoet, Cox and Olupona 1996: 42). Our findings in the description of Osun myths in the New World should throw more light on the significance of Yoruba in other parts of the world (Bourdillon 1996: 150).

Many African students learn about the influence of Yoruba religion in the world during their studies in America, Europe and Asia (Platvoet 1996: 65-87; Oosthuizen 1989: Drewal 32:160-185; Barret 1968). Ironically, the continued existence of Osun in the New World is news to most Yoruba religious students who have not travelled outside the country. For it is inconceivable that a Yoruba religion could exist outside the

African continent for so long and that is shaping the belief and faith of other world religions. For this reason, scholars have jointly called for a "dramatic increase of information and communication which is the hallmark of globalizing modern society" to re-establish historical links that exist between older forms of religions (Platvoet, Cox and Olupona 1996: 3-8).

The presence of a Yoruba religion in Europe and in the Americas has left indelible impacts on western cultures and religions (Okpewho, Davies, Mazuri 1999: 34). Just as tobacco, cassava, peanuts and maize, which were introduced to Africa by the early Portuguese, have been incorporated into African menus, also the African worship that has found its way into the New World has become an American religion (Bascom and Herskovits 1959: 3). As the American and European cultures, education, ethics and products influence the African countries, so does the Yoruba religion affect the shape and scope of religion in Europe and America. This is one reason why the descriptive mythological method is a suitable one to connect and evaluate the degrees of the impartation of a Yoruba religion in America.

A. How did the Yoruba get to the New World?

As we have read in the previous chapters, in 1840, the goddess Osun helped the people of Osogbo to win a series of tribal and religious wars over their enemies (Hugh 1999: 356). These battles affected men and women in Yorubaland (Akinjogbin 1998: 122). There are documented accounts of wars that ravaged the Yoruba land in the past. Examples of such wars that the Osun deity was deemed to have helped to win were "the successful repulse by Abeokuta of the Dahomi attack in 1851…" (Ajayi and Smith 1964: 32; Parrinder 1951/1976: 97). During these periods of inter-tribal wars, most of the captives were sold to white slave merchants and they became slaves, while others were killed in battle. Some of the people now referred to as Afro-Americans are descendants of the Yoruba people who survived wars, shipwreck, sicknesses and diseases of land and sea. Consequently, the Yoruba people who made it across the Atlantic were essentially those who had been sold as slaves to the European slave traders.

In the era of the slave trade, some Yoruba people, ironically, betrayed their kinsmen by selling them into slavery and exchanged them for commodities such as salt, alcohol, spices and gunpowder. While it was not an easy migration for those who were sold into slavery as they were stripped naked and transported in ships to the European and American countries, it was a booming business for the slave merchants. According to Thomas Hugh, in his book *The Slave Trade; The Story of The Atlantic Slave Trade: 1440-1870*, the slave coast was soon sending about sixteen thousand slaves a year to the Americas; which was a large number of African population then (Hugh 1999: 356).

Unfortunately, thousands of them did not make it to America because they died in transit, while those who did, ended up working in the plantations. Incidentally, the victims of slavery and the slave trade were mainly from those tribes which were resident near the coast and maritime areas (Klein 1978: 599-609; Kopytoff and Miers 1977). Slavery continued up to the nineteenth century (Inikori 1999: 51). Even, after the signing of a treaty to prohibit slavery in 1815, vessels were still carrying slaves from Yoruba towns to Europe and America.

B. Osun in the New World

Some time ago, certain people were threatened by the contributions of the Yoruba religion in the New World, therefore they insisted that the worship of Orishas must be abolished in the New World. The critics did not take into consideration that African-American people are descendants of African slaves just as their European counterparts were immigrants in the Americas. Christianity, Islam, and other religions are immigrants' religions in the Americas as well. This was not the first time that people attempted to abolish the African worship in the New World. Patricia Monaghan writes, "the Christianity of the slaveholders demanded that the old gods be left behind and that only one divine story be told" (Monaghan 2004: 191).

In an effort to erase the African religion from the memory of the slaves, the slave masters wanted them to become Christians. It was difficult for the African slaves to embrace Christianity with the cruelty of slavery. From fear of revolution their masters turned blind eyes to their practice of ritual and sacrifice activities. Sarah Cameron states that "although the slaves were ostensibly obliged to become Christians, their owners, anxious to prevent different ethnic groups uniting, turned a blind eye to their traditional rituals" (Cameron 2004: 425). Those who became Christians frequently attended the African initiated worship and festivals. It was impossible to erase the worship of African deities totally from their minds. Instead of eradicating the worship of African deities, corresponding ideas were created to substitute those they were used to in Africa.

Of the many religions, gods, goddesses, rituals and sacrifices that came through the storms of persecutions and still exist today is Osun. Here is the public, concise knowledge of people of her.

1. Osun as Orisa

Orisha **or** *orisa* is the name for all divinities that had their origin in the Yorubaland. Osun's identity and myth in the New World are similar to the rest of the Yoruba *orisa*. The Yoruba recognize over 400 divinities, but "barely two dozen regularly receive tribute at the rites known as *toques de santo*" (Cameron 2004: 425). Osun represents them all more in the New World. Joseph M. Murphy and Mei-Mei Sanford in their recent publication stated how important Osun is in the New World.

> As an orisa, Osun offers what all the orisa offer: the good things in life, health, wealth, and love. She can be one orisa among many, or many orisa in one. She can even be the Supreme Being. Many priests and priestesses of Osun address her as Oluwa, "My Lord." Amid the titles and attributes of Osun that Jacob Olupona offers us in the beautiful invocation that begins his essay is the stunning declaration that, for the singer, Osun is "my Olodumare," my God Almighty. Here Osun is recognized as God, the author of destiny and divinity's source (Murphy and Sanford 2001: 7).

Clearly myths of Osun sustain the Yoruba spirituality in the New World (Murphy and Sanford 2001: 1). She is an embodiment of different aspects of virtues and personalities. Apparently, Osun has been promoted to the same level as God in Yoruba belief which many Yoruba people would find hard to accept.

2. Osun as a Saint

Osun as a saint is the New World applied title. Patricia Monaghan argues that by people calling Osun a saint contributed to her existence in the New World today. She said that the Africans adopted "new celebration, new symbols, and sometimes new names" for their divinities for the sake of continuation of their worship (Monaghan 2004: 191). The appellation "saint" appeals to the modern minds in the name of religious identity.

In the New World Osun's name was changed and she was given new symbols and new images as part of her worship. Osun became a saint. She crossed the denominational and cultural borders (Murphy and Sanford 2001: 7). Osun was identified with Our Lady of Pleasure, Our Lady of Carmel, and as Mary Magdalene in the African Center of Saint George. She is Our Lady of La Caridad the patron of Cuba (Monaghan 2004: 192).

This adaptation of a Yoruba divinity was not limited to Osun, but was done to other Yoruba gods in America. This dynamic equivalence of personality of Osun in the Americas sustained her memory in the New World.

In another account, "the daughters of Osun go to mass at Our Lady of Carmel just as the daughters of Abraham did" (Platvoet, Cox and Olupona 1996: 274). People are allowed to worship Osun and still go to mass in a Catholic Church. The Yoruba people freely practised their religious ceremonies in these *cabildos* which served as club houses. The combination of the Catholic pantheon and Orisha elements gave birth to what is called Lukumi worship, even though the European–American Catholic members could not comprehend how the Yoruba could worship Osun and Jesus Christ at the same time.

In Yorubaland, the celebration of the Osun festival is held during the rainy season, so "how to localize ceremonies linked to a certain rhythm of nature and society in a country having a different seasonal rhythm became a challenge" (Platvoet, Cox and Olupona 1996: 274). The African diaspora found ways to adjust their worship of Osun to a more suitable time and place in the new geographical settings. In dealing with different geographical settings, people and countries, let us briefly look at Osun worship in Cuba.

5
Osun in Cuba

This is one of the myths of Osun that survives in Cuba. It is full of symbols and images that demand our attention in this study. Such myths as cited below are "a story with culturally formative power that functions to direct the life and thought of INDIVIDUALS and GROUPS or SOCIETIES" in the New World (Hexham 1993: 153). A myth was told to describe how the goddess became a river.

> It happened this way: flirtatious Oshun desired the god Chango, who was already mated to the goddess Oba. So Oshun, never [one] to be discouraged where love was concerned, concocted a plan to steal Chango for herself. One day, Oshun pulled a nasty trick on Oba. Claiming that Chango preferred her cooking, Oshun shared her secret: that she cut off parts of her ears and put them in the dishes. It was really only mushrooms that Oba saw floating in the soup, but they looked enough like parts of ears for the goddess to be convinced. The next time Oba cooked for Chango, she cut off a whole ear and mixed it with the food. This, alas, made the dish revoltingly foul-tasting, and Chango was even more revolted to see his mangled mate. When Oshun arrived to gloat, Oba attacked her. The two goddesses turned into rivers, and where their waters meet, there is always turbulence (Monaghan 2004: 192).

Myths such as the above are parts of the Yoruba oral narratives that have sustained Osun worship in Cuba for many years. Slavery and slave trade brought the Africans, especially the Yoruba, to Cuba and they had no freedom of worship. Over a period of time, they became the most influential group of the African people in Cuba (Cameron 2004: 425). The myths enhanced their spirituality. How the Yoruba people came to Cuba is not the focus of this book but our aim is to explain how the people retained the worship of a Yoruba divinity through the retelling of religious stories and by attaching religious importance to regular objects.

When the Africans arrived in the New World as slaves they met similar religious groups with similar myths and religious practices. This encouraged them in their spiritual journey. They met "the religions of the Taino and the Cuna and other Native Americans, who had their own panoply of symbols and their own pantheon of divinities" (Monaghan 2004: 191). This provided an encouragement for them to continue the worship of the African divinities in the New World.

The population of Yoruba among the African slaves was so high that they formed a major group in Cuba, making them noticeable in the country.

> In Cuba and Brazil, the relocation of those from Oyo and Ketu led to an American resurgence of the cults of Obatala, Eshu, Ifa, Osanyin, and Ogun and to a revitalized worship of such river goddesses as Yemonja – rechristened Yemaya in Cuba and Xemanja in Brazil – and Oshun, the Cuban Ochun (Matibag 1996: 53).

It is written that Osun worship in Cuba can be traced back to the Yoruba people of Nigeria. The memory of Yoruba worship, magic, ritual, sacrifice, music, dance and a sense of roots sustained her worship in diasporas (Warner-Lewis 1999: 22). There is an element of truth that "Many Yoruba customs and expressions that no longer exist in Africa persist in Cuba" (Considine 1958: xvi). If we may add, there are a lot of inventions attributed to the Yoruba religion in Cuba which did not have their origins from the Yorubaland.

Fidel Castro, on one occasion, remarked that, "We are Latinafroamericans!" (Matibag 1996: 1). He implied that the African religions have greatly colored Cuban religions and cultures. Though, initially, the African religion was a forbidden one on the island, it eventually became a formidable force in the life of the people. It was no longer a secret religion as Mason pointed out:

> The historical experiences of slavery and repression created an atmosphere of secrecy as the followers of the religion tried to protect themselves from the social forces that threatened them. Under slavery in colonial Cuba, the practice of the religion was technically illegal, and accusations of "witchcraft" could mean imprisonment or death (Mason 2002: 9).

In spite of the rough beginning and threats made against slaves, the Yoruba religion flourished because of the survival of its myths in Cuba.

In the academic circle, it has been difficult to explain the specific connection of a Yoruba divinity to a specific town in Nigeria as we have done here. Therefore, scholars have tied all of the Yoruba divinities with each other under the term *orisha*. But the new development is that the Hispanic cultural elements are parts of the Yoruba divinities. Matibag noted that, "indeed, as developments in religious forms have perhaps most clearly demonstrated, the amalgamation, synthesis, symbiosis, or crossing of diverse West African and Hispanic cultural elements in the American setting produced a new religious culture" in Cuba (Matibag 1996: 1).

At present, due to mass immigration of Cubans into the United States of America, Yoruba worship is coming to the United States. However, Badejo has observed that the cults of Yoruba gods and goddesses are not as popular in the United States as they are in Latin America (Badejo 1995: xxiv). As Yoruba descendants in Cuba migrated to the United States, some came to "the Sea Islands, Georgia and other regions in the south of the United States; from Bahamas Islands; among the Cape Verde folks who migrated to the New World made the United States their home" (Herskovits 1943: 1). In the twenty-first century, there has been an increased interest in worshipping African gods due to the inflow of refugees and immigrants directly from African countries into the United States. People from the Yoruba kingdom met with the Cuban immigrants who were descendants of African slaves and recognized their common origins and belief in worship. Each party was excited to share their acquired oral knowledge with the other.

The memory of Yoruba gods and goddesses are fresh in people's memories and the Cubans have recollections of what their grandparents shared with them (Matibag 1996: 52-53). Surprisingly to the new immigrants from Africa, Osun is not the only Yoruba goddess that survived in Cuba. Yemaya, which the Yoruba call Yemoja exists in Cuba (Matibag 1996: 61). Yemaja and Olokun are companions of Osun in the Old and the New World. Myths of these three goddesses are interconnected. The Yoruba people in Cuba believed deities such as Oshun, Yemoja, Olokun and Oloosa protected the African slaves on the seas when they were bought and brought to the New World. Out of gratitude, reverence and awe, the Yoruba in Cuba have good memories of Oshun and other divinities (Matibag 1996: 62-64).

A. The Africans as Lucumi

Over a period of time, the Yoruba in Cuba have gone further in welcoming other tribes from other African countries to freely worship Osun with them. Unlike the Yoruba in Osogbo where the majority of her devotees are Yoruba, the majority of Osun worshippers in Cuba are not of Yoruba descendants who came from Osogbo. All Yoruba from different towns came together in Cuba as one. Africans usually discriminated against each other when they were in African villages, but overseas, they became brothers and sisters. Black Americans and African immigrants still show mutual bonds in the twenty–first century.

Yoruba love speaking their language in religious worship of Osun. A priest is said to have acted in the following ways in Cuba as it is being done in Osogbo today.

> He drops the shells and counts those that land with their serrated "mouths" up. Oché is the name of this odu (Lu.), or divination figure. 'Maferefún Ochún. Thanks be to Ochún. Oché speaks of the blood that runs through the veins (Sp. *La sangre que corre por las venas*) (Mason 2002: 16).

Similarly, during Osun worship, Yoruba people in a community often gather together as one family. The Egba, Egbado, Ijebu, Ijesa, Awori, Ketu, Ekiti, Oyo, Ife, or Kwara in Cuba call themselves Lucumi as a united brotherhood and sisterhood. Lucumi or Lukumi is a Yoruba phrase known as '*oluku mi*' meaning "my friend". Another interpretation is "*Olokun mi*" (my dear one). It is a phrase used in exchanging greetings among the African descendants in Cuba.

Secondly, Lucumi is a reference for the Yoruba and Nupe (Takpa) people who were born in Cuba as slaves. The Yoruba descendants began to use it as one of the words to refer to people who have a common source of origin.

> Thirdly, Lucumi is a language that unites the people of African descent in the New World. Lucumi, a dialect of Nigerian Yoruba, is still spoken by a number of Cubans. In Trinidad, as in Jamaica, Hindi is still important to most of the descendants of migrants from India, at least for special purposes, while the same is true of Tamil in Martinique (Mintz 1989: 23).

Speaking a common language in a foreign country is a way of retaining religious and cultural memories. Language promotes relationships, history, culture and aids the spread of religious myths.

Fourthly, 'Lucumi' was used among the Negroes of Mexico. A

mystery has been traced to the Yoruba form of greeting, known as *oluku mi* 'my friend.' It is more than likely that the reasons and explanation given above are an answer to the mystery of the word "Lukumi". It is important to note that the Yoruba people in Brazil preferred to be referred to as *Nago,* a name given mainly to the Fon people of Dahomey the neighboring country of Yorubaland. The name the West African groups bear abroad was not as important as a deep brotherhood and sisterhood that bound them together as one.

In Cuba, the Yoruba language is known as *Anago*, which is another name for a Yoruba group in the Yoruba kingdom (Matibag 1996: 24, 53; Bastide 1960: 94, 116). It is possible that the majority of slaves in Cuba are members of the *Anago* areas of Yoruba tribe because the *Anago* people live very close to the Atlantic Ocean which would have made them the most common victims of slavery. The Anago version of the Yoruba was also easier to learn than the Oyo pronunciation of Yoruba language. No wonder the majority of slaves in Cuba called themselves Anago (Verger 1976). Pierrre Verger rightly argues that the Yoruba is known as Nago in Brazil, and they are called Lucumi in Cuba. The only people who are called *Anago* among the Yoruba are those who live in the Idiroko border of Nigeria. These are small Yoruba groups with a distinct dialect. Yoruba has close to fifty different dialects, but the majority of them understand each other.

One of the features of the Yoruba religion in Cuba is that it blends in well with the Cuban religions and with many other West African religions, with which it shares different attributes. The religions of the Bantu, Ewe-Fon, Mandinga, and Carabali are similar to the Yoruba religion. It was rightly noted "that Cuban culture in the first half of the twentieth century could accept and assimilate African-based mythical and religious thought" because of the spirit of brotherhood and sisterhood that people had (Matibag 1996: 11).

B. African Religion in Cuba

Initially, African social and religious elements were held "equally hostage to the dominant white culture" and this feeling of insecurity "led to an aggressive cultural nationalism" (Okpewho, Davies, Mazuri 1999: xvii). When slavery was abolished, it gave the people in Cuba religious freedom as well. Many Yoruba in Cuba then returned to their religious and cultural practices. In their search for the lost cultural and religious identities, Sidney Mintz and Richard Price said that the Africans in Cuba created a new social structure which was grounded on African traditional beliefs (Okpewho, Davies, Mazuri 1999: xix). Antonio Benitez describes how the African elements became one of the most cherished points of cultural reference in Cuba (Okpewho, Davies, Mazuri 1999: xvii). Davis Evans also explained how the African musical instruments, which are social instruments of enjoyment, became the accepted musical instruments for the musicians. This eventually contributed to the survival of the African religion in Cuba (Okpewho, Davies, Mazuri 1999: xvii). A Nobel Prize winner, Wole Soyinka, in the twenty-first century also states that Yoruba music is rich in traditional myth and poetry (Badejo 1995: 117; Soyinka: 147).

C. Yoruba Religion in Cuba

The spirit of Osun is recognized as important in the Santeria tradition. De La Torre said the word Santeria is from the Spanish word *santo* (saint), and it means "the way of saints" (De La Torre 2004: xi). The use of the term started as a pejorative reference to religious worship such as Osun. The Catholic clerics in Cuba use Santeria to refer to what they considered "a heretical mixture of African religious practices with the veneration of the saints" in Cuba (De La Torre 2004: xii). The term became "popular in 1940s in the Cuba cities of La Havana and Matanzas where large concentrations of Yoruba settled" (De La Torre 2004: xii). In Cuba, "the initiates of Santeria are *santeros / santeras*" (Bjoring 1988: 107). They believe greatly in the activities of the spirits.

The African worshippers see the new movement as a way of expressing their spirituality within the Catholic majority of the time. Today, Santeria is flourishing in Cuba, Latin America and in the United States of America (Bjoring 1988: 105). Santeria and Voodoo are similar in origin and beliefs for both religious groups borrow a lot of ideas from the African religion.

Yoruba beliefs and practices formed the major aspects of Santeria. Kenneth Anthony Lum states that, "it is their pantheon of deities or *orisha*, and the legends (*pwatakis*) and customs surrounding these, which form the basis of the syncretic Regla de Ocha cult, better known as Santeria" (Cameron 2004: 425).

It is interesting to note that Santeria has a different name. Today, "Santeria is non-sectarian and non-proselytizing, co-existing peaceful with both Christianity and the **Regla Conga** or **Palo Monte** cult" (Cameron 2004: 425). This is the original nature and attitude of Osun worshippers in Yorubaland.

D. Osun Worship in Cuba

The slaves worshipped at Catholic altars, but in their minds they were worshipping the African gods. Osun welcomes the use of candles. Monaghan states that "various rituals emerged to honor her, ranging from candles lit in Christian churches to possession by her spirit in midnight dances" (Monaghan 2004: 192). These are new innovations, but whatever symbols and materials that makes Osun happy are employed in her worship and remembrance.

Osun has multiple images in Cuba. She is a diviner, dancer and the one who can be anything to anybody.

> Isabel Castellanos shows us that five roads of Ochun in Cuba take their devotees down different paths in understanding the goddess and themselves, ranging from Ochun Ololodi, the serious diviner, to Ochun Ibu Kole, the powerful buzzard, to Ochun Yeye Moro, the gorgeous dancer. There is indeed one Ochcun but she is the unknown source of the different roads, and their destination (Murphy and Sanford 2001: 7).

To the Yoruba in Osogbo, Osun is known for her involvements in religious, political, and economical affairs of the people. For the Yoruba in Cuba, "Ochun has been called the Yoruba Aphrodite: or the goddess of the Oshun river in West Africa and sister of Yemaya" (Matibag 1996: 64). Osun is known to have territorial authority over most West African towns and villages.

In Santeria, Osun is a spirit. She is a spirit who possesses power. As a being, she retains her personal name and identity among other Yoruba spirits in Cuba. She appears to people and communicates to them. She can be contacted through diviners and mediums. Her worshippers use pebbles, water, rituals and incantations during divination. Drums, dances and songs increase the possibility of Osun spirit possessing people during worship.

1. Oceans, Rivers, Lakes

In Cuba one of the symbols of Osun is water. Monaghan reiterates the point by saying,

> Water is preeminently the symbol of Oshun. In Voudoun, when she 'rides' or possesses a dancer, the woman will make swimming motions, jangling her arm bracelets as she does it, while others welcome Oshun's appearance with shouts. Altars to her may hold shallow dishes of water; her festivals often connected with bathing in rivers, lakes, or seas

(Monaghan 2004: 192).

People make use of water day by day. It is an essential commodity to survive in life. The rivers, lakes and oceans of the New World have become emblems that illustrate the power and being of Osun in the Yoruba communities. Fresh water is a necessity. All the living beings live on water. Osun the owner of fresh water reminds the people that Osun has the power to sustain living things.

Osun's authority and symbol is not limited to water, it covers the areas of "beauty, love, and sexual desire" (Badejo 1995 1995: 10-11; Matibag 1996: 64). Osun is very beautiful with, "dark skin is as sleek as velvet" (Waldherr 2007). She is thought to have an irresistible image. Osun's loveable attraction draws men and women to her. Human beings and gods want to be her lover. A myth survived in Cuba about how Osun's mother jealously kept her away from men who were crazy to marry her:

> Men from miles around would come to Oshun's house when she was young, begging her mother for Oshun's hand in marriage. No one knew the young orisha's name, but her beauty was renowned. Her mother turned them all away until one day, yearning for the hordes of would-be suitors to leave her alone, cried, "Enough! I will consent to a wedding to any man who can figure out the name of my daughter!" Among the men was the great diviner, Orunla; he was confident the oracle would reveal to him the beautiful young orisha's name. But try as he might he could not get them to tell him, and he eventually asked his friend Eleggua the trickster to help.
>
> Eleggua hid by the door of Oshun's house. Days went by, but the mother was careful never to mention her daughter's name. One day, however, the old woman became exasperated when the girl spilled a mixture of herbs and water on the floor. "Oshun!" she cried. No sooner had he yelled Orunla marched triumphantly up to his beloved's mother

and demanded to wed Oshun now that he knew her name (Miguel 2004: 75)

People make the heart in the logo of Osun (Monaghan 2004: 193). In spite of Osun's later marriage to Sango, Osun encourages fidelity in marriage. Osun's personality encourages and promotes romance between lovers. The beach and maritime areas are places of romance. She is the goddess of love.

> Ochun rules the heart and gives people the human love they need. She is the basic connection between people that keeps society functioning, and in many of her stories she solves a problem by making contact with another supernatural power. Through their "rule" of different domains of human endeavor, the orichas affect the lives of their followers (Mason 2002: 95).

Orisa Osun loves water and the vicinity is a place for romance with nature and people. As a couple is joined in marriage, the next thing they pray for are healthy children. After the wedding, Yoruba people expect the new couple to have children within the first year of marriage.

As we have mentioned in part one, Osun gives children to barren women who visit her at the river (Castellanons 2001: 39-40). She works with other divinities to fulfill this task (Castellanons 2001: 42). The power of fertility, reproduction and enjoyment of sex belong to Osun. Yemoja, Oba, Olokun and Osun are Yoruba goddesses who cure infertility of men and women. Osun, in particular, is recognized as the owner of female genitalia and the female eggs.

2. Love, Beauty and Sex

As quoted above, Osun is in control of beauty, love, and sexual desire in Cuba. The heart's becomes the emblem of Osun (Monaghan 2004: 193). The heart desire of women and men is to find the love of their life who intends to bear children for them. A goddess who controls the quality and quantity of beauty, love, and sexual desire cannot be easily forgotten among those who aim to have children. Osun is a goddess of beauty (Lawal 1974: 239).

Osun is the goddess of love and lust. Karen Tate stated that "Her experience in the arts of lovemaking have earned her the name La Puta Santa, or Whore-saint, as well as Puta Madre, Mother-whore" (Tate 2006: 132). Osun became the goddess of the prostitutes because she is thought to be a prostitute too. She encourages freedom of self-expression and satisfaction. Stephanie Palmine reported that, "mostly in Cuba, Chango may reveal himself a loudmouthed braggart, Ogun may turn into a wanton destroyer and Ochun into a fickle prostitute willing to sell her affections to the highest bidder" (Palmie 2002: 194). Explanations had been given for the reasons behind her prostitution as, "she is more accurately the sexually liberated woman who gives pleasure to herself and of herself when she so desires, reflecting the true meaning of the Virgin Goddess who is powerful within herself" (Tate 2006: 132). The Americans have made Osun into a feminist advocate and the Yoruba morals became relative in the New World.

Miguel A. De La Torre shared her experience with Osun worshippers as follows: "When I was young, I would often witness brawny men who were possessed by Oshun begin to display seductive feminine characteristics, while dainty women possessed by Oggun would become belligerent intimidators" (De La Torre 2004: xi). This form of sexual movement is not condoned in Osogbo today. People have probably been educated over the period of time while the Africans in the Americas still allow the tradition in their worship.

Anybody who is involved in prostitution in the Yoruba community is seen as a disgrace to humanity. Yoruba make a distinction between two kinds of beauty, *ewa-ode* "bodily beauty," which is more of an outward appearance and *ewa inu* "beauty-in-character." The most precious and desired beauty is the latter one which has an intrinsic quality. In Yoruba thought, too much beauty could be a sign of being evil or being connected to wicked spirits. Osun worshippers have been accused of not only prostitution but of homosexuality.

> Mythologically, especially in Cuba, styled as the seductress of various male gods, Ochun further exemplifies, not just a moment of irresistible sexual attraction, but female sterility. Some divination proverbs style her as a divine prostitute, but, more important, perhaps, she stands for "all that is sweet in life," including, not just sexual pleasure, or self-enhancement through wealth, but the treacherous sweetness of sugar (Palmie 2002: 282).

In the footnote the author goes further to say, "at least today, male devotees of female deities, particularly Ochun, are pervasively rumored to be at least latent homosexuals. In the inimitable and untranslatable words of a babalawo with whom I worked in Miami…" (Palmie 2002: 282). This would be a serious bone of contention among the Yoruba who adore Osun of Osogbo. Homosexuality is an abomination among Yoruba people.

3. Osun's New Names and Personalities

Osun accepts different personalities and names in the New World. Osun became the Lady of Charity in the Catholic churches (Castellanons 2001: 40). She is also known as Our Lady of Cobre among the Catholic Church Saints. The people worshiped Osun in Catholic churches as they openly declared that Osun is a daughter of Olofin. Osun's houses became holy symbols of spirituality to the Yoruba descendants in Cuba.

The worshippers still retain the African attitude of dancing, singing, and celebration during Osun worship in the New World. Whenever the

Africans are holding their worship services, sounds of Yoruba music fill the air. People use different kinds of musical instruments in celebrating Osun. Examples of these materials include stones, planks, and locally made drums. They improvised many of the materials that their parents were using in Osogbo. One of the reasons for the worship of Osun is that the people were able to express their emotions in worship. For the Yoruba descendants, the Catholic worship was too slow and dull. In Santeria worship, the worshippers offer a lot of frankincense, oil, and candles to "St. Osun" and dance until the spirit of Osun possesses them.

E. Osun in Santeria

The Yoruba made different images of Osun. Benitez Rojo traced the similarities of Osun icons in Cuba saying that "the Spanish Virgen de Illescas as Yoruba Ochun Yeye Moro and the Taina goddess Atabex or Atabey are similar in appearances" (Matibag 1996: 11). It was difficult to differentiate the personality of Osun from that of other icons. One would require the help of spiritual leaders who are familiar with the icons to differentiate one image from another. The interesting thing about the above-mentioned divinities is that "these three divine personalities did not however merge into one but maintained their separate identities as three-figures-in-one-entity" (Matibag 1996: 11). In a religious setting where Osun worship does not dominate the history, culture, ethics, and government of the people as it does in Osogbo, it is easy to confuse the personalities and characters of Osun with other divinities. Two or more divinities may be similar in appearance and attributes, but their functions and beings may be opposite. This point supports a religious argument that "a syncretic artifact is not a synthesis, but a signifier made out of difference" (Matibag 1996: 11). As Osun stood out as a deity from Yoruba, she could not be merged or submerged into Christian saints. No doubt, myths contribute to the continuity of the Yoruba culture and tradition in Cuba. By devoting themselves to the Yoruba religious images, the elements from West African religion and Catholic belief systems converged to transform Cuban religion (Matibag 1996: 11). Osun worship developed in Cuba as the Africans concealed it from the authorities (Okpewho, Davies, Mazuri 1999: 34). Yoruba men and women came with the ideas and beliefs of their gods and traditional folklores. The Yoruba language, myths, proverbs and religious worship were firmly established in Cuba. Hence, polytheistic, animistic beliefs, ritual meditating and practices gained ground in Cuba.

Among all the African peoples in Cuba, the Yoruba were very committed to their ancestors and gods (Bastide 1971). They looked for every way to sustain their interest and knowledge of their ancestral religion in Cuba. They practice initiation rites, spirit-possession, sacrifice, divination, magic, and casting of spells using the name of Osun and other Yoruba gods. Osun worship is growing in Cuba (Badejo 1995: 13).

During the early period of the Yoruba in the New World and their subsequent migration to the Americas, the people had to accept the reality of give-and-take in practicing their religious beliefs. In Cuba, for example, Osun's names, pronunciations, beliefs and rituals underwent some changes. Cross Sandoval explains more about these changes that almost made Osun worship into a "made-in-America" religion (Matibag 1996: 57). In Cuba, Roman Catholicism changed the nature of the Osun religion to such an extent that the Vatican finally recognized her as one of its saints. Her names, identities, and ontological status, have been adjusted to Catholicism. It is written, "the Virgen de la Caridad del Cobrel, Ochun, became Cuba's patron saint by decree on May 10, 1916, under Pope Benedict XV. She is celebrated on her feast day, September

8, in Santiago de Cuba" (Farrow 1996: 14; Matibag 1996: 57-58). Thus Osun entered into official records of the Church. Her position of patron saint is an important one. As Osun was incorporated into the family of the saints, worshippers gave her new attributes that she did not have in Osogbo. Osun becomes the goddess "who owns and loves money," attributes that were never part of her image in Yorubaland (Matibag 1996: 58). Money was not a means of trade before slavery in Yorubaland. People were doing business using trade-by-barter until the beginning of the eighteenth century.

1. Osun' Favorites

Miguel A. De La Torre expressed the bias of the media to Santeria in the Americas by saying "But all too often, when compared to the normative Eurocentric manifestation of Christianity, Santeria is presented to the world through Hollywood movies and the news media as idolatrous, dangerous, or a product of backward people" (De La Torre 2004: xii). Whereas Santeria is the worship of Yoruba deities in the Catholic churches where icons are used as educational-religious items (Matibag 1996: 52-53).

Osun has different icons that represent her in worship. The icons of Osun are in private homes and churches in Cuba. Diedre L. Badejo assesses the significance of the African icons by saying, "thankfully, the key to African worldviews remains within reach. The primary knowledge base which is the iconography of African images persists like African American spirituals..." (Badejo 1995: xv). This popularity of African icons positively revived other religious activities such as rituals, myths, prayers, and dances.

i. Images: The icons of Osun in homes and churches are constant reminders to the worshippers.

> In an abstract, decontextualized sense, Ochun is understood as a young, beautiful, light-skinned black female oricha who has many lovers and

is extremely fond of perfumes, fans, mirrors, jewelry, and all kinds of finery. She loves music, dancing, and celebrates the joy of living. She is also skilled in the arts of seduction and lovemaking. Ochun Yeye-Moro and Ochun Ibu-Akuaro are the "best examples" of this prototypical Ochun (Castellanons 2001: 35).

As a young divinity in the Americas, Osun will always remain young in that context. That quality accorded her an opportunity to be one of the Cuban Catholic saints. As she was known in Haiti, Osun is a mulatto with a dark skin (Owusu 2002: 27). She has been compared with Venus in Taurus (Kaldera 2004: 141). Her youthfulness is winning her more followers from the teenagers.

In Cuba, Osun is known as Our Lady of Charity, Lady of Cobre. Like other saints, Osun loves music, dancing and to celebrate life. There are poems, with the wordings related to the sea and old river, summarizing where Osun came from. She is known as the source of fresh water. A non-androgynous being, Osun is a female virgin and this statement reminds us of how the *Arugba* Osun in Osogbo is expected to be a virgin. Virginity proves one's character, chastity and self-control and is worth emulating by young people.

Osun is dark in complexion in Cuba because they know that she is originally from Africa. She is as black as coconut sweets sold at the markets. In Cuba, the appearance of any fire beetle is a reminder for people of Osun.

Osun and Olofin, another African goddess, work closely to produce fresh water for people and their farms. Osun waters the plantations of sugar and the grain fields. The palm-trees are woven as her dress. The coves and inlets of the river are under the command of Osun. As she controls the Osogbo River, Osun controls water sources in the New World.

ii. Sexual Activities: Cabrera in *Yemaya Ochun* sees Osun as "the Lover, the personification of sensuality and love, of the force that drives the gods and all creatures to seek out one another and to unite with one another in pleasure" (Matibag 1996: 64). Osun is portrayed as a divinity who encourages sexual relationships among human beings and also in the spiritual world. Osun's appearance is irresistible to men who were her contemporaries. Her beauty lured two Yoruba divinities to fall in love with her. She married more than one Yoruba god, Chango (Shango), and Orunmila (Badejo 1995: 2, 56). The myth states that:

> The oricha Ochun and the oricha Oba were both married to the kingly deity Chango. Oba was unhappy because she felt [the] Chango spent more time with Ochun and not enough time with her. She went to Ochun and asked how she might entice Chango to pay her more attention. Ochun replied that Chango loved her cooking and that is why he spent more time with her; she also suggested that Oba make a soup from her ear because the excellent taste of the soup and the devotion of giving an ear would surely win Chango's affections. Oba made the soup and served it to Chango who commented on how good it tasted. "What is in it?" he asked. "My ear," replied Oba as she removed her head covering to reveal the bandaged ear. Chango was repulsed and fled for [from] Oba. It is said that he never forgave her (Mason 2002: 53; Ecun 1885:253).

Osun's first known lover was Orunmila (Castellanons 2001: 41). And later, Osun became the favorite wife of Sango (Matibag 1996: 65). Osun's rival in marriage was Oya, the goddess of Yoruba rivers. Shango eventually divorced both Osun and Oya because of their constant fights and jealousy at home. With all of Sango's power and ability to control thunder and lighting, he could not control his two beautiful but quarrelsome wives. This story becomes a powerful reminder for the worshippers of Osun in Cuba, and a repetition of it sustains worship of Osun.

The stories surrounding the marriage of Osun to Orunmila also spread in the New World. As we have heard, Orunmila is a Yoruba god who is in charge of divination, wisdom, knowledge, medicine and healing. Orunmila gives vision to *babalawo* "priests," *onisegun* "herbalist," and *adaunse* "juju man." A number of slaves in the New World continued practicing or at least visiting the herbalists. Yoruba slaves patronized them because they thought that western medicine could not cure or heal all of the Yoruba diseases in the foreign land. Spiritual problems require spiritual attention which the herbalists could deal with.

iii. Color: In the New World, Osun and her devotees have a favorite color: yellow. Worshippers of Osun usually made an effort to have yellow as part of his or her daily dress (Mason 2002: 71). Shopona, the god of smallpox and the dry season, shares the use of yellow color with Osun (Verger 1976: 171). Whenever a slave dresses in a pure yellow it is a statement that the person is either a follower of Osun or Shopona. As Osun's favorite color is yellow, Orunmila's color is green (Matibag 1996: 119). In the history of Cuba, at one time the use of color led to public disputes. On September 4, 1933 the revolution against Machado raised a conflict on the use of yellow and green.

iv. Number: The use of special numbers also became important in Osun worship in Cuba. Osun perfect number is five, "and five are the diaphanous scarves she wears around her waist" as typical of her images (Matibag 1996: 65). Devotees are reminded of Osun when the number five is mentioned at social or religious circles.

v. Food: Regarding food, Osun devotees in Cuba think that Osun loves honey and pastries more than any form of food (Matibag 1996: 65). She also loves watermelon and yellow pastries as part of her dishes (Mason 2002: 16). She loves sweet pastries with sweet baked oranges and chicken (Ocha'ni lele 2003: 221). We should note that the above mentioned items are not part of her favorite menu in Osogbo.

But to be on the safe side, worshippers in Cuba still consult the priests to know what to offer Osun during services.

> After this intensification of the realities of life, the diviner offers a method to transcend the situation. "Ochun wants partridges," he tells her. Each oricha has particular foods: Ochun is partial to hens, fish, partridge, eggs, shrimp, oranges, and fine pastries. The conflicts are further intensified by the deity wanting something (Mason 2002: 25).

Some of the Yoruba special food that the Cuban worshippers give to Osun in worship is *olele* (Ocha'ni lele 2003: 222). *Ole* or *olele* is the mixture of blacked-eye peas, eggs, red pepper, garlic, palm-oil and tomato sauce.

Osun had special plates for her sacrifices. She "owns *albahaca*, or basil, which is used in many magical and medical mixes" (Matibag 1996: 65). Her food must be served in a clean calabash. Her devotees have to build an altar or throne for her where they must place the plaza of fruits (Ocha'ni lele 2003: 220). They are obliged to be careful in their presentation of sacrifice, "the omo-Ochun or child of the goddess prepares for her a favorite dish... made from shrimp, watercress, and almonds. Other favorite foods [she likes are] she-goat, fish, hen, and beans" (Matibag 1996: 65). Osun's food comprises sea food and bush-meats. She even has to share some of her favorite menu with other divinities:

> The orichas share together at the level of ritual practice, but this detail usually indexes some mythic explanation as well. Ochun and Aganyu share castrated goat, and santeros explain this fact by pointing to their strong association with the river; they are of the same place and eat the same food (Mason 2002: 75).

This is a kind of African union of deities in a foreign land. Goats are regular meat of the Yoruba people and they offer goats as sacrifices to their divinities.

vi. Materials: Osun also adores smooth round stones from the river shore. She is known to be associated with small rivers, as stated here: "associated primarily with the flow of sweet (as opposed to marine) water, Ochun's powers are also felt in movements of circulation, not just of earthly waters, but of blood and money" (Palmie 2002: 281). Water is a natural element that reminds worshippers the personhood of Osun in the New World, so is the flow of the blood serves as her reminder too (Mason 2002: 4).

In addition to the items from rivers, the flow of blood and money was an innovative idea of Osun worship in Cuba. This was a new thought added to the worship of Osun in Cuba (Matibag 1996: 65). The Yoruba-Cubans are well organized and more careful in preparing Osun's sacrifices. As she is a goddess of the river, most of her sacrificial items are from the river and few other domestic items are added to Osun's sacrifices. She is therefore the goddess of the land and the sea. Osun's beauty is directly credited to the kinds of food she eats from sacrifices offered to her by people (Badejo 1995: 10-11).

Osun likes using mirrors and jewelry. Monaghan says, "But Osun is also the playful goddess who loves, above all else, beautiful jewelry and mirrors – the later so that she may better admire her beauty" (Monaghan 2004: 192). Improving self-image is one of the popular ideologies of the people in the Americas. Osun becomes their role-model and idol. Jewelry and mirror are essential symbols of beauty in the New World.

vii. Poetical Verses: In reverence of the personhood of Osun, her devotees still use Yoruba words and phrases in daily prayers and incantations. Here is one of the descriptions of what goes on at Osun's shrine:

> She asks for the blessings of the ancestors. She names one, then another, and then another. She asks for the blessings of the orichas and makes a long prayer to Ochun. Then she cuts off the braid. Many

> people repeat this process, each one invoking their ancestors and orichas before cutting away at my hair (Mason 2002: 5).

These regular prayers are in the form of recitation or incantation which could also involve the cutting of one's self with a razor blade (Abiodun 2001: 25). Sociologist Fernando Ortiz wrote articles on the influence of the African religion on Cuba's art, religion, and language. Lydia Cabrera also indicated that Africans had influenced almost everything in Cuba with their lifestyle (Matibag 1996: 1-3). This influence has been called different things by different people including "cultural transplantation, diffusion, and synthesis" to name a few (Matibag 1996: 1-2).

In addition to the sociologists' observations, Jose Sanchez-Boudy also published works on Afro-Cuban poetry. Cubans are the whitest in complexion among the people of the Caribbean islands, but the black people's influence on the island's culture and religion are immeasurable. It is widely accepted that most of these African elements came from the descendants of Yoruba slaves. Joseph Murphy's work on Santeria and African spirits in America suggests that the Yoruba divinities in American religions are in different forms and shapes (Matibag 1996: 8-9).

The *orisa* in the New World have myths supporting the spiritual activities of their worshippers. Every step must be guided according to the dictate of the divinity. Sarah Cameron states that "for every *orisha* there is a complex code of conduct, dress (including colour-coded necklaces) and diet to which his or her *hijos* must conform, and a series of chants and rhythms played on the sacred *bata* drums" (Cameron 2004: 425). By abiding with requirements of the *orisa* Osun one could experience religious phenomenal such as spirit possession.

2. Spirit Possession and Initiation in Osun

Initiation rites, spirit possessions and consulting divinations are common practices in African religions both in the Old and in the New World (Badejo 1995: 13). African myths, folktales and proverbs form the conceptual frameworks for sustaining these religious experiences.

One of the common features in Osun Worship is spirit possessing the worshippers. It is usually the next experience after a devotee is initiated into the Osun religion. De La Torre stated that "during possession, gender lines can blur as male orishas spiritually possess female bodies and vice versa" (De La Torre 2004: xi). This is one of the religious experiences that men and women have in common. Other religious phenomena are the initiation rites and the practice of divination. Spirit possession in a secular setting would be spectacular for those who had never witnessed it before. People manipulate the spirit-world for their own financial gain or social recognition (Mason 2002: 7).

3. The Yoruba Language in Osun Worship

One of the factors of spirit possession in Osun worship is music and drumming. Yoruba music and drums follow the lyric of Yoruba language. Osun worship is usually in Yoruba. Initially, the use of Yoruba language helped the early Africans to conceal their intention of Osun worship from their masters (Mason 2002: 9). As it is written, "some of the oral texts themselves serve as refractions of the knowledge brought by those who had crossed the Middle Passage [sea]" to the New World (Warner-Lewis 1999: 12).

Every Yoruba word, phrase and sentence is rich in meaning and it takes a deep understanding of it to know what is being said. For instance, the Yoruba word *igba* could mean time, rope, two hundred, or garden-egg; it depends on the context. Where one places accents in writing and on tone or emphasis in speaking determines what one means in that context. In most cases, the context determines the meaning of each Yoruba word of a sentence.

At the early stage of Osun worship in Cuba, the slave-masters did not understand most of the Yoruba language. It therefore was a tool of communication that concealed the truth of African religion from other people. It was a means of religious expression among the people and with their divinities both in singing and chanting incantations to their gods (Matibag 1996: 8-9). Yoruba songs and music are not merely for entertainment but full of religious and ritual messages.

Messages and customs are encoded in the beating of drums. Thus the Yoruba could secretly communicate to their members and their gods. It is one thing to understand the Yoruba language, but it requires training of ears to understand the language of the drums. Before the arrival of foreigners in Yorubaland, the sound of special drums often warned the community that something was about to happen in the village or town.

Drums and drumming are part of worship that divinities enjoy. Gods and goddesses have favorite drums. It is honorable to understand and to be able to play Yoruba drums. This special ability and training can make one a celebrity in the community. Yoruba would say that one *gbo ilu* "hears and understands drums". It means one's understanding is deeper and better than many people in the crowd, for drumming communicates secret messages, most especially, the talking-drum otherwise known as *gangan* or *iya-ilu*.

Yoruba drums come in different sizes and different forms. A set of drums and drummers could be playing different sounds, beats, regulating the moves of the dancers. This is one of the beauties of Yoruba religious festivals (Bascom and Herskovits 1959: 56). Combinations of beautiful tones, rhythms, movements, and graphical gestures add meaning to Yoruba religion and worship. John Roberts has argued that African oral narrative, especially in drums and dancing, contributes to the continuation of the African religion in the New World (Okpewho, Davies, Mazuri

1999: xix). As we have discussed earlier, *bembe* is the favorite drum of Osun.

Drums speak African, a united language in Cuba, partly because they are essential instruments in African entertainment. The language of the drums is a means of keeping bonds tight in a foreign land. Europeans who loved music were also drawn into the group.

A later challenge was that the grandchildren and great-grandchildren of the Africans did not understand the Yoruba language well enough to understand the language of the drums. Only a few of them could understand little phrases and sentences of their parents' language, and none of them could speak the Yoruba language fluently (Matibag 1996: 53). Where the Yoruba language had failed in reminding them of the African religion, African drums and music still generated interest in it. The drums and music bring the Yoruba in Cuba together in the worship of divinities.

In addition to the Yoruba language, and talking drums, is ritual dance in Cuba. Ocha'ni lele described how the Osun dance is in demand. "In Oche, Oshun may want the client to give her a huge party with lots of music. The bigger the party, the greater the blessings this Orisha will bestow" (Ocha'ni lele 2003: 2003). Yoruba people love to party. Either social or spiritual, initiation or christening, everything is marked with a huge party. One should not be surprise that Osun expected a huge party from somebody who is expecting abundant blessings.

In summary of the importance of Osun in Cuba, she became the divinity of lakes, rivers and the ocean. It is reported that "Ochun, for instance, eventually lost among Cubans her identification with a specific African river – no longer relevant in the new setting – and expanded her role as the "owner" of all rivers" (Castellanons 2001: 36). She is also remembered because of her interest in African drums (Castellanons: 42).

6
Osun in Brazil

Heike Owusu paints the picture of Osun in Brazil. Osun is known as Oshun, Oxum, Ezili or Erzulie in Brazil. Osun is the Loa-Gods of Candomle, which is similar to Voodoo and Santeria. Osun in known in Candomble as having the follows particular symbols:

> *Attributes*: Goddess of love and of creative powers, mistress of abundance and passion – beautiful, seductive, young.
>
> *Sacred places*: Mountains, running waters
>
> *Symbols*: Jewelry, mirror, fans, gold, little bells, parrot, peacock, quail, clams, hawk
>
> *Day*: Thursday
>
> *Colors*: Coral-red, yellow, green
>
> *Number*: Five
>
> *Favorite food*: Cake, oranges, cinnamon, honey, melon
>
> *Planets*: Venus, waxing Moon
>
> *Ritual Place in the house*: Bedroom, kitchen
>
> *Salutation*: Ori Ye Ye O (Owusu 2002)

Before we discuss these myths of Osun in Brazil, let us take a moment to talk about the Yoruba in Brazil.

In the last section, we detailed how Osun became a saint of the Catholic Church in Cuba in the tradition of Santeria. The papacy recognized her and Osun became one of the most popular saints in Santeria (Matibag 1996: 58). This section of our discussion is aimed at understanding the significance of Osun worship in the tradition of Candomble (Farrow 1996: 12).

Bjoring indicated that "*Candomble* is a name given to a variety of African traditions which were established in Brazil in the nineteenth century. Bahia, or Salvador de Bahia, is the center of Candomble" (Bjoring 1988: 108). Language, music and icons contributed significantly to African worship in this religious tradition. The African myths and symbols sustain the tradition in Brazil. How the tradition started is not known but "Iya Nasso, a Negro priestess, was instrumental in organizing a Candomble community in Bahia in 1830" (Bjorling 1988: 108). She contacts the spirits of Yoruba gods for people who are in crisis.

A. African Myths in Brazil

African myths, rituals and practices exist in Brazil today as by-products of slavery. One of the myths states that "Ochun felt sorry for Babalu-Aye and told Orunmila to smear her best honey on the walls of Olofi's place. When Olofi tasted Ochun's honey he immediately wanted more. Ochun responded: "I will not give you any more of my honey unless you bring Babalu-Aye to life." God complied and Lazarus was resurrected thanks to Ochun's intervention" (Castellanons 2001: 38). This is an example of the kind of myth that people of Yoruba descent believed in. It has been said that "this faithfulness to African cults" kept the slaves together as one (Verger 1976: 470). Social transformation and relocation could not rob the African people of their solidarity in Brazil.

Africans in Brazil gained religious and political freedom through a series of public revolutions and demonstrations. It got to a point where the religious and political authorities in Brazil perceived Africans to be a nuisance. It is written that, "the black population and above all the Africans, were however a source of disquiet: there were a great many slaves and they were felt to be a menace. In 1792, the Haiti revolt had led to the victory of the blacks; in Brazil, it had filled the whites with panic and the blacks with hope" (Verger 1985: 10). The whites became more suspicious of the Brazilian blacks and mulattos. The whites knew that they had the potential to form revolutionary groups. It is stated that "the judicial enquiries that followed the 'Male revolt' in 1835 gave insight into certain problems of co-existence of the African slaves and freedmen in Bahia and showed certain aspects of their division" (Verger 1976: 459). Two of the major causes of disagreement between the whites and the blacks were religions and the inhumane treatment people of African descent received from the Brazilian authorities. However, one university took a positive step to reconcile the different minority groups on its campus. On the cover of the brochure produced by the University of Bahia for the International Conference of Brazilian and Portuguese studies, were the names of Bahia saints, the Virgin Mary, Sango, Sopana and Osun (Verger 1976: 168-171). We should point out that Sango, Sopana and, of course, Osun, were divinities that had their origins in Africa.

B. The Yoruba in Brazil as *Nago* Community

As we have examined the treatment of Africans in Brazil, we need to focus on how the Yoruba were identified in Brazil. The Yoruba population contributed to a high percentage of blacks in Brazil. The mulattos, who were the children and grand-children of African-Brazilian couples, helped to ease the religious tension seen initially in Brazil. As a sizable minority, descendants of the Yoruba and the mulattos started coming together to worship the African-initiated divinities. These people were mixing African beliefs with the Catholic religion.

The people who initiated this new form of religion were mostly descendants of the Yoruba, which people referred to as "Nago". The word "Anago" was a reference to a Yoruba dialect group from the south-west of the kingdom. "Anago" was too difficult for the Brazilians to pronounce and they shortened it to "Niga".

Yoruba people in Brazil came from different parts of Yorubaland, including: Ketu, Ijebu, Awori, Egbado, Egba, Oyo, Ife and Ibadan. In Brazil, all of these groups of people became one Yoruba nation from Africa. Initially, the Yoruba who had resided close to the border of the Republic of Benin were called *Anago*, but eventually *Niga*, a derivation, became the name of all black Africans in America.

Lucumi is another name given to the Yoruba in Brazil (Matibag 1996: 24, 53). For in a place such as Bahia, the former capital of Brazil, the Yoruba worshipped the divinities of their ancestors known as *orisha*. This group of people address themselves with the term *lucumi* meaning "my comrade" (Verger 1976: 1680). The word *Lucumi* has its origin in a Yoruba word. At such meetings the people reminded themselves of the past, encouraged themselves in their present struggles, and hoped for a better future.

1. Yoruba Descendants as Farmers

The high percentage of blacks in the population of Brazil contributed to the country's socio-religious development. The African religions survived chiefly in the sugar-growing regions of the northeast. In the sugar plantations, Yoruba slaves had freedom of worship and enjoyed holding small group meetings. The same is also true of the cattle-raising areas of Brazil where the Yoruba people acknowledged the "moral values and the intellectual richness of their ancestral beliefs" as they wandered in the natural habitats (Platvoet, Cox and Olupona 1996: 331). These people had enough time to meditate on the "questions of right and wrong, true and false" as they worked in agricultural settings (Bourdillon 1996: 149).

Yoruba people in Brazil were not only found on farm settlements, indeed most of them were living in cities. City life offered them the freedom of anonymity. Cities were for everybody. A city environment weakens social control of the blacks. Africans enjoyed the company of the crowds which lived in cities.

2. Yoruba Cults

It was reported that in Brazil, "the Nago-Yoruba of the Ketu 'nation' met in the church of Barroquinha and formed the brotherhood of Nossa Senhora da Boa Morte, which came out in a procession every August 15. It was in the shade of this church that the first participants in the cults of African gods from this Ketu nation met (Verger 1976: 465). As time went by, different Yoruba cults grew in different parts of Brazil as they had opportunities to come together more often for religious meetings. The Yoruba held *ipade* "meetings" of small groups after the general meeting. The churches in Brazil allowed Yoruba groups to meet after Catholic services to share their common cultural and spiritual interests, which, of course, were African in nature. Life in the city gave the Africans the opportunity to hold meetings regularly and they became recognized groups.

Yoruba people had money to spend on refreshments during traditional meetings and festivals. At the time, the number of blacks in Brazil was growing rapidly, approximately three and a half million were counted towards the end of slavery. This number grew considerably from the eighteenth century due to the arrival of shipment of more people to mine gold in Brazil. The abolition of slavery gave them freedom to relocate to better places.

Since the first day of their arrival in the New World, Africans' religious, cultural and social heritage started spreading in Brazil. Their heritage survived alongside the Portuguese religion, culture and social institutions. For a group with strong ancestral foundations, such as the Africans, it was difficult, if not impossible, to forego their faith for a new one. The majority of the slave masters had no interest in converting their slaves to Christianity. They were indifferent to their spiritual life. The slave-owners were liberal in allowing slaves to follow their religious convictions. However, Catholic priests and converted black Africans tried to convince their black African colleagues to become Christians. In 1713, some individuals attributed the failure of the spread of Catholicism to a lack of resident chaplains who could do a follow-up on the small number of converts.

C. Challenges Encountered By Yoruba Worshippers in Brazil

During religious festivals, there were occasional recollections of the unfavorable conditions of slavery their forefathers had suffered. This generated anger among the Yoruba in Brazil. This bad feeling between Yoruba tribes and memories of inter-tribal wars sometimes hindered free worship among the African people (Verger 1976: 460).

Few Catholic leaders attempted to impose their religious convictions on loosely connected African people. The Catholics welcomed the African slaves in the church. Fellow Africans discriminated against the Africans who genuinely became Christians. The "Africans in Bahia were often separated from one another by religious matters" (Verger 1976: 460). Their levels of commitment to Christianity and African religion were different. There was evidence of religious discrimination among the converted slaves and their descendants. It is believed among some devoted Christians that when one is converted to Christianity, he or she must totally reject ancestor worship.

African converts regularly met in worship and to talk about their newfound faith. Organized African-Christian groups borrowed ideas from the Freemasonry practical administration guidelines so that they could be recognized by the government.

The Brazilian government made idol worship easy for the Africans there. Part of the government policy was to promote cultural diversity among its citizens. Africans quickly seized the government's given opportunity to organize themselves according to their religious interests and tribal origins.

It was annoying to some people hearing African slaves' songs repeatedly and loudly. At work, individually and collectively, the Yoruba slaves enjoyed singing religious music and worship when they remembered their homeland. As they worked, the African slaves sang and danced to their native songs which motivated them to be productive and fulfilled. In situations where the slave owners were noticed to be very strict on religion, the Yoruba would pretend to be singing Catholic songs whereas they were honoring their African divinities. It is written that when they were singing and dancing:

> The whites believed them to be dancing to the glory of the Blessed Virgin or the saints, but the Virgin and the saints were more [significant] than masks. The steps of those ritual ballets, whose significance quite escaped the masters, ...The music of the drums abolished distance, bridged oceans, momentarily bringing Africans to life and creating a communion of men in one end and the same collective consciousness, in an exaltation that was at once frenetic and controlled (Badejo 1995: 54).

Most African descendants used various available objects and instruments to make music to their gods and goddesses (Verger 1976: 470). African religious music used naturally gifted voices in making melody to the divinities. One scholar stated that in Brazil he saw that the Africans were committed to their performance to a point of "savage enthusiasm" in their songs and dance (Verger 1976: 471). "Savage enthusiasm" was a negative phrase to describe the mood of the African descendants in Brazil. A savage enthusiasm is a genuine spiritual expression in worship and this deep involvement in worship is missing in Catholicism.

In spite of the lenient Brazilian government policy, the African "nations" in Brazil were too few in number to have a widespread influence on leadership or to own buildings, unlike other nationalities which had fraternities, monasteries and sanctuaries. The Brazilian civil government did not know that as they were promoting a peaceful religious and cultural co-existence in Brazil, they were also contributing to the growth of the minority religions. It was not too long before they realized what they were doing in promoting paganism and "in 1768 the existence of true African shrines was denounced" as illegal (Verger 1976: 470). But it was too late to undo their mistakes for African religion had put down roots in the social, political and religious structures of Brazil.

The Africans had adapted themselves to a new social setting. Although the New World superstructures were foreign to them, they functioned well within the religious parameters. Back in Africa, the Yoruba believed in a family lineage, clan identity, village system and hierarchical structures that helped them to behave ethically (Afolabi 1974: 44-58). In Brazil, the religious institutions adopted some African hierarchical system of government at home and followed the leadership of their masters as a normal lifestyle. As time went by, African religion in the New World was changing its appearance as one generation passes the beliefs to the next generations.

D. The Yoruba Religion in Catholic Faith

The type of Catholic faith that the Portuguese brought to Brazil encouraged the growth of the African religions side-by-side with Christianity. They formed an alliance as both groups acknowledged the subjects of ancestors and saints regularly featured as one in their faiths. Catholicism favored and revived the veneration of saints who shared similar profiles with the African ancestors. Particularly, Catholic superstitions were compatible with African religious practices. Unlike in Europe where the veneration of saints was monitored, the Brazilian Catholics experienced less supervision from the Vatican. Due to various reasons, Brazilians were isolated from Rome, therefore, people did things the way they thought best. In fact, Africans had more freedom to worship their ancestors under the leadership of Catholics immediately after the abolition of the slave trade than when they were under the monitoring of their slave-masters. Religious symbols, values and the ideas of the Catholic Church and the Yoruba religions were used interchangeably in Brazil.

1. Yoruba Churches Operating Under the Catholic Faith

As the slaves saw the similarities, Catholicism later encouraged African-Christians to start their own parishes. This made it easier for Africans to practise their faith in their own way within Christianity. This allowance eventually led to the growth of independent African churches (Okpewho, Davies, Mazuri 1999: 386). Gradually, pure African rituals and beliefs were being discontinued in Brazil as an independent religion but "in transforming the African cults, the church, without meaning to, often helped them to survive" by letting traditional African culture be itself in Christianity.

African culture is as practical as Christianity. As with other religions, African cultural values were deeply rooted in the moral codes of black Africans in Brazil. Their mental attitudes, modes of behavior and emotional patterns were revisited during birth, adulthood, marriage and burial ceremonies. These sorts of rites of passage are transitional stages of life, which owe their origins to African religion.

Another way in which African religion had an influence in Brazil was in instilling the belief in magic and religious formalism. The whites were fascinated by the Africans' magical powers. The Portuguese migrants were as superstitious as the African slaves, but the Africans contributed to the sustenance of religious magic in Brazil. Both the African slaves and the Portuguese immigrants had many things in common; they were foreigners and they had lost contact with their homelands. Both groups found solace in the practice of magic. Magic and magical performances are not religious acts as such, but are the means to manipulate human minds, and magic enhanced the image of Africans in Brazil.

2. Osun in Yoruba Worship

Osun worship continues in Brazil because the Yoruba myth and culture jointly create traditional etiquettes in the mind of the African descendants in the region.

i. Authority and Power: One leading factor in the growth of African religions in Brazil is the African gods' and goddesses' claiming of authority over domestic materials, seasons and natural forces. It was pointed out that,

> Some of the general characteristics of these are respected. Shango rules over the rocks, Ogun over iron, Oxun over sweet water, Yansan over bamboo (because of her connection with death, symbolized by bamboo), Oxossi over forests (where he hunts), Omolu over cemeteries, Exu over crossroads, Yemaja over the sea. But gradually these deities rise from the plane of natural forces to the plane of moral ones (Platvoet, Cox and Olupona 1996: 328).

The Yoruba divinities ruled and were remembered in almost all aspects of creation and behaviors in Brazil. Sango, according to the perception of the Yoruba people, is in charge of thunder and lightening. The slaves often remembered Sango as their god and their divine father whenever it rained. His efficacy was so powerfully felt that the Yoruba believed that Sango could strike dead anybody who was a thief in the community. Ogun, on the other hand was believed to be the god of iron and he protected those whose symbols of trade were connected with metalwork. Ogun became so powerful that it took Osun to get too close to him. One day she lured Ogun to her side.

> Women offered themselves. But no one could lure the hermit from his hiding place. Ochun decided to try. She went into the forest, intoned a song, and began to move her body to the music. Ogun watched her from behind some bushes. Enchanted, he soon showed his head in order to see better. Ochun came quickly to his side and daubed his mouth with honey. Little by little, Ogun came closer and closer to Ochun, who continued dancing and giving him honey to eat (Castellanons 2001: 38).

Who dare say Osun is not powerful. Her seductive power got Ogun and even *Exu*. *Esu* is a devil in Yoruba understanding. He is also the minister of 'justice'. He punishes the wicked people and ultimately kills those who continue in their wickedness before they reach their full age (Verger 1976: 470).

ii. The Priests (*Babalawo*): Another religious factor that sustained the Yoruba religion in Brazil is the presence of the *Babalawo*, "the Ifa (oracle) priest". The Yoruba in Brazil recognized the *babalawo* "priests" as their religious leaders. Priests maintained the use of the Yoruba language in communicating with divinities and in prescribing incantations for clients. It is widely believed that the gods and goddesses listen to the priests any time they invoke the divinities in the vernacular. In Yoruba prayer systems there is *oju odu* and two hundred and forty sub-servants called *omo odu* (Olabimtan 1974: 50). The *Babalawo (Ifa* priests) made voodoo for the Yoruba in Brazil as they practice the Yoruba prayer custom by this they reminded African descendants of the history of the religion.

From time to time, the parties involved in the incantations would sing Yoruba songs praising their ancestors, gods and goddesses, most especially during the making of the sacrifices and rituals. Their attitudes to the divinities were positive as they sang traditional songs and used traditional instruments during the rituals.

In Brazil, Osun and Yemanja collaborated in blessing female reproductive systems. Yoruba religions cooperated with other African faiths to form the bedrock of the Yoruba-Brazilian practices

> Ochun and Yemaya, then, are equally essential to motherhood, since the former owns the organs that make conception possible while the latter attends to pregnancy itself and to nursing and caring for the children. Motherhood is equally distributed between these two orichas (Castellanons 2001: 42).

Osun and Yemoja are partners in Brazil. For instance, "Yemanja, the well-known Abeokuta orisha who is considered the mother of all other orisha, has been confused with the Virgin of the Conception" because the people thought of them to be one (Verger 1976: 171).

The use of the color white as a symbol has played the same role in linking Obatala, god of creation and Mother of Mercy as one family (Lawal 1974: 242-243). Yellow color connects Osun to the Virgin of Charity of the Catholic Church, which was not so from the beginning (Verger 1976: 171). In conclusion, African religion is embedded in the history of Christianity in Brazil.

At the beginning of this discussion we cited Heike Owusu's summary of the symbols of Osun in Brazil. Osun is Oxum, Ezili or Erzulie in Brazilian Voodoo. Her attributes and characteristics are outlined as follows:

> *Attributes*: Goddess of love and of creative powers, mistress of abundance and passion – beautiful, seductive, young.
> *Sacred places*: Mountains, running waters
> *Symbols*: Jewelry, mirror, fans, gold, little bells, parrot, peacock, quail, clams, hawk
> *Day*: Thursday
> *Colors*: Coral-red, yellow, green
> *Number*: Five
> *Favorite food*: Cake, oranges, cinnamon, honey, melon
> *Planets*: Venus, waxing Moon
> *Ritual Place in the house*: Bedroom, kitchen
> *Salutation*: Ori Ye Ye O (Owusu 2002: 25).

Some of the symbols we found here are: mountains, little bells, parrot, peacock, quail, clams, hawk, Thursday, coral-red, cakes, oranges, waxing Moon, bedroom and kitchen. Her associations with these symbols add meanings and memory to Osun worship in Brazil. One group that we need to state a mythological narrative behind is the animal category:

> One of her symbols is the peacock, but the other is the vulture. There is a legend that in her youth, Oshun volunteered for a hideous duty that all other orishas shied from, and they openly doubted her ability to do the job. She accomplished it at a great personal risk by taking the form of a peacock. She flew a long way to give a message, but in the process her beautiful Venus – bright feathers were burnt off and she returned as ugly vulture (Kaldera 2004: 143).

This myth makes sense in connecting the importance of vulture and peacock symbols in Osun worship. Symbols in myths are helpful in the continuation of Osun worship. Feather forms part of head-dress in Yorubaland. It is a part of ritual dance customs. It is a symbol of beauty and beautification (Waldherr 2007: 79).

In Brazil, the symbols and myths of Osun are similar to those found in the rest of the New World. Monaghan indicates that "In Brazilian Macumba, Oshun shows her sensuous nature by wearing jewels, holding a mirror, and wafting a fan. Altars hold copper bracelets and fans, as well as dishes filled with Omuku (onions, beans, and salt)" in remembrance of Osun (Monaghan 2004: 193). In addition to other symbols, fans became one of her favorite symbols in Brazil.

The influence of Osun in Brazil had spread to the United States as recorded by Pomba Gira. In New Orleans some of the Vodou divinities share the "traits with several *orixas,* particularly sensuous aspects of Oshun (Oxum) and Oya" (Gira 2004: 82). This particular work is arguing for the contribution of Osun to the gay, spiritual, bisexual, and transgender practices among the African-Americans.

142 Portrait of Osun

144 Portrait of Osun

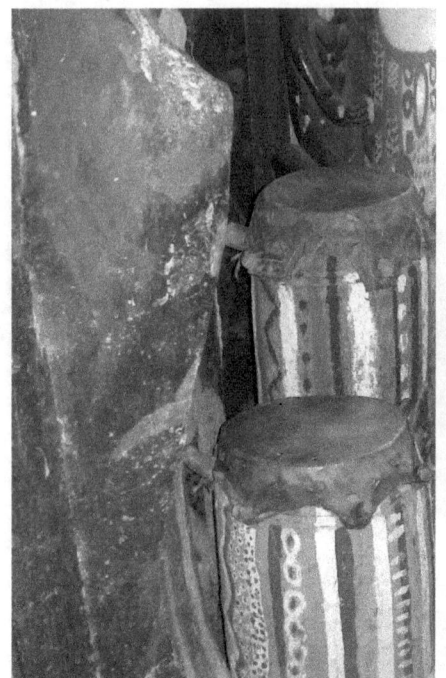

Portrait of Osun 145

146 Portrait of Osun

Portrait of Osun 147

7
Osun in Trinidad, Jamaica and Haiti

A. Osun in Trinidad

The island of Trinidad is "situated at the southernmost end of the Caribbean archipelago which stretches from Florida in North America to Venezuela in South America" (Lum 2002:1). As early as 1790, Trinidad was one of the Spanish colonies. Slaves from Africa and the second generation from the French West Indian islands formed almost 50% of the population of Trinidad (Lum 2000: 218). Starting from 1777 to 1834 slavery was fully established in Trinidad. After the emancipation of the slaves, the ex-African slaves immigrated to Trinidad in 1839.

1. Yoruba Religion in Trinidad

In addition to the presence of Osun in Cuba and Brazil, we have evidence of Osun worship in Trinidad. It is written: "The Orisha religion began in Trinidad only during the last century, and its primary components were borrowed from the Old World" (Houk 1995: 115). This is buttressed by the comments made by Melville J. Herskovits about the significance of African worship in Trinidad by saying that:

> The Bahian post-possession phenomenon termed were... since discovered in Trinidad by Espinet and Eduardo... is a major contribution of Afroamericanist research to Africanist studies. The phenomenon of possession is ubiquitous in West Africa, if not in all African religion. It has often been recorded and in these descriptions the states preceding possession, and possession itself, are invariable treated. But the experience of coming out of possession has thus far been quite overlooked (Herskovits 1966: 21).

Specifically, the Yoruba language and religion have their footprints on the island through the efforts of free African immigrants who came from

Martinique, Guadaloupe and French Guiana to Trinidad (Lum 2000: 201-202). The number of Yoruba people outnumbered the rest of the tribal groups in Trinidad as indicated below:

> In the case of Trinidad we have to recall the significant number of free African immigrants who arrived during the nineteenth century after emancipation. A distinctive Yoruba identity continued among some Trinidadians well into this century, and Maureen Lewis suggests that little-known Yoruban words continue to be used between close friends (Littlewood 1993: 87).

Yoruba deities and divinities were kept alive with the use of the Yoruba language. James T. Houk said, "The deities of the Yoruba religion in southwestern Nigeria and the Orisha religion in Trinidad and the beliefs associated with them, for example, are often virtually identical" (Houk 1995: 53). Idols served the purpose of icons in connecting Yoruba worshippers with the reality of African divinities. A closer scrutiny of religious activities in Trinidad yielded evidence of Osun worship. It is written:

> Yemoja, is the symbol of motherhood and the fullness of the sea; Oya, the hurricane, air, the lungs; and Ochun, symbol of female beauty and ruler of the veins of the body. Because of the prominence of West African Yoruba among slaves and immigrants brought to Trinidad, the name of Shango, a king of Oyo state, became generic to Orisha worship, the state religion of Oyo and its politically affiliate city-states (MacGaffey 2000: 405).

Originally Yemoja, Oya and Ochun had their beginnings in Yorubaland. Jointly the three played major roles in the lives of Africans in Trinidad. Among them, Osun was the symbol of beauty and caretaker. She is believed to monitor the body's blood circulation that resulted in making one look and feel good.

i. The Context: Trinidad is a unique historical setting for practicing Yoruba religion. It is a very small island discovered by Christopher Columbus in 1498. Initially the Spanish made Trinidad a home for slaves from Africa to work on the plantations (Simpson 1970: 107). Eventually, in 1783, Spain opened Trinidad to non-Spanish immigrants to settle (Simpson 1970: 112). Finally, in 1797, Britain took over the island and made it one of her colonies. In the eighteenth and nineteenth centuries, many African people came to Trinidad through immigration, colonial and slavery activities.

In 1835, Negro slavery was abolished in Trinidad (Simpson 1970: 108). In 1855, the Caribbean Indians received the last group of African immigrants who wanted to resettle in Trinidad. Most of the emancipated slaves, especially the Yoruba, came from other nearby islands to resettle in Trinidad because of the favorable geographical setting and weather. Consequently, Trinidad became the best place for the freed African slaves.

The weather and vegetation were similar to the West African tropical region. The African immigrants introduced most of their cultural and religious beliefs to Trinidad. African songs became part of their daily entertainment. Trinidad became the land of African music and divinities. All African divinities lived side by side with each other:

> Two minor Shango powers in Trinidad with whom our Mother Earth has certain affinities are African Queen and Oshun (now Mistress of the Ocean). A number of female water deities are to be found among the Afro-Caribbean cults, some of whom appear to be variants of Yemanja; other powers have attributes which are similar to hers and which may have been derived from her or have contributed to her current form. Thus, the Bakweri liengu water spirit, creolized as Mami Wata, was found under this name in the Guianas where a slave revolt appears to

have been fought under her name; also known as Minje Mamma (Emanja Mother?) her cult was characterized by the Europeans as some unspecified 'obscene worship' (Littlewood 1993: 140).

Political rallies and political activities were how the immigrants voiced their opinions. As an extension of Osun's attributes, she became the Mistress of the Ocean. Her identity became larger, she was not just in charge of a river as in Osogbo but she was in control of the ocean (Castellanons 2001: 42).

As in Osogbo, Osun was thought to be too particularly interested in certain areas of Trinidad. Roland Littlewood, in his footnote noted that "Oshun was the presiding power of a small Trinidadian-Grenadan group known as Emanja's Children" (Littlewood 1993: 140). In Trinidad, it was not easy to forget the significance of African religion in such places.

Professor George E. Simpson was one of the few scholars who had studied the Shango cult in Trinidad. As one of the earliest authorities on the subject of Afro-American religious influence in the Caribbean, he published a work on Shango in 1965 where he argued that Shango cults in Trinidad combined elements of Yoruba traditional religion, Catholicism and the Baptist faiths (Simpson 1970:11). Originally, the Baptist faith is rooted in evangelical and in the believers' church tradition. It was hard to believe that African religion could have anything to do with the evangelical beliefs, because they are committed to fundamentals, dogmatic and strict statements of faith.

ii. Music in Yoruba Religion: One could get information on most of the Yoruba divinities and historical past from the lyrics of the Yoruba songs. African songs provide "effective and informational" themes on "their traumas and religious belief" of their experience in Trinidad (Bascom 1972). The effects of slavery and religion gave musical inspiration to the surviving generations in Trinidad to accept their fate and get on with life

(Platvoet 1996: 55). In addition, the African musical groups in Trinidad revived peoples' interest in magic and voodoo through their performances (Simpson 1970:108). The settlers derived greater satisfaction from African music than they did from other social involvement (Simpson 1970: 108).

The Yoruba religious worship took a new shape in Trinidad. Whenever the Yorubas were celebrating a particular festival or divinity, they would take time to recognize all other divinities. For instance, whenever the Yoruba people were observing the Sango festival, they would simultaneously offer sacrifices to Obatala, Oya and other Yoruba divinities (Simpson 1970: 103). An additional dimension of African worship in Trinidad is the practice of astronomy, especially in urban settings (Simpson 1970: 100).

In the urban areas of Trinidad, African religious worship is more sophisticated than in the villages. The form of African worship has changed to the extent that one may wonder whether the devotees of Sango found in the cities of Trinidad are actually from Africa. It is interesting to note that the Trinidadians who participate in Yoruba cults perceived themselves as "Yoruba people," "the Yoruba nation," "orisha people," or "African people" (Simpson 1970: 85). Like Osun worship in other parts of the New World, Sango devotees encouraged people from different nations and cultural backgrounds to join them in worship (Simpson 1970: 85).

2. Osun Worship

During Osun worship, drumming, dancing and singing uplifted the people to predispose them to spirit-possession. This religious phenomenon could be traced back to the African practice (Badejo 1995: 54). In Trinidad, Sango devotees would march slowly around the interior of the shrine (Simpson 1970: 26). The beat of the drum is what controls the movements of the dancers. In the process, all the dancers bow in front of the drummers to maintain eye contact with the drummers.

People respond differently to the sound of the drums and music during religious festivals. Those who are spiritually possessed would shake their heads, shoulders and jerk their legs vigorously at the beat of the drums. Their depth of ecstasy during the ceremony is an indication that the power of Sango is in action (Simpson 1970: 20). This phenomenon is called *egun Sango* 'spirit possession' in Yoruba language. The possessed person could be in the state of possession for hours or days depending on the will of Sango (Simpson 1970: 27). It is noted that the possessed person "can put one after another ... lighted wicks in his mouth without being burned" (Simpson 1970: 28). The possessed person is normally and completely out of the physical realm and such a person may have no feeling of pain. Herskovits explained that the cultural, psychiatric and social aspects of possession affect the believers' world view and moral ethics (Simpson 1970: 29). Bastides, in his own analysis, states "that Brazilian blacks make a distinction between (i) possession by the gods and (ii) possession by spirits of the ancestors and Eshu" (Simpson 1970: 31; Bastide 1960: 520). In that setting, those who are possessed by the evil spirits are normally wicked people. It could also be an effect of psychological problems that make them possessed. African worshippers on both sides of the Atlantic still witness and experience spirit possession.

Yoruba people believe it is possible to secure spiritual power from the divinities during the period of spirit possession. Like Osun, in Trinidad, Sango has good and evil powers available to those who wish to use them in their "fights for survival" (Simpson 1970: 22). Some practitioners use the good power to secure healing for the sick, getting favorable judgment in difficult civil cases in court and so forth. In connection with Catholicism, "one prominent Sango leader said that it is difficult to get "good" powers to perform "work" during the Christian period of Lent because the gods and goddesses are engaged in answering the prayers of the Catholic Church members (Simpson 1970: 22). This, according to their belief, is because Yoruba divinities are very much involved in attending the prayers and fasting sessions of the Catholic Church during Lent. Yoruba divinities form a part of the body of saints in Christianity in Trinidad. During Lent, men and women who use icons in religious worship make use of Yoruba divinities as icons.

i. **Sacred Centers and Forests**: The African religion in Trinidad is closely connected to Yoruba religion.

> The Orisha religion, by far the most eclectic and syncretic of the three, began as a transplanted West African (Yoruba) religion and through time gradually took on Catholic, Protestant, and Hindu elements, in that order. Its complexity and eclecticism can be attributed, at least in part, to colonial activity in Trinidad (Houk 1995: 37).

As we have seen with the Osun grove and Osogbo and Osun rivers, Sango's stories contributed to the continuation of Yoruba worship in Trinidad. Sango religious centers in Trinidad are sacred places where people place offerings for their dead relatives (Simpson 1970: 23). Sango, as we have discussed earlier, was one of the husbands of Osun. Sango centers in Trinidad resemble the shrines that we had seen in the grove of Osun in Osogbo. In Trinidad, Sango religious centers are full of *pierres* "thunder stones", which people believed to have fallen from the sky during rainy periods. In the Yoruba language, these stones are called *okuta Sango or edun ara*. These small smooth stones are kept on white plates in the shrines in the Chapelle (Simpson 1970: 32). The Chapelle is a small building, about twelve by twelve feet, which is a place of Sango worship (Simpson 1970: 35). The thunder stones are the main weapons of Sango and if found on the street, people always return the stones to the Chapelle. It is an accepted fact that Sango fights his enemies with these stones whenever he is provoked on a matter.

In addition to the sacred stones in the Chapelle, there are also "statues and lithographs of the saints, crucifixes, candelabras, candles, vases of artificial" flowers and other necessary ritual paraphernalia. Other important paraphernalia is stored in the leader's home. These include ritual clothing such as "robes, shirts, and turbans for men, and dresses, head wraps, and beads" (Simpson 1970: 36). These materials are innovations of the Sango worshippers overseas.

Sango's sacred stones, as mentioned above, are purified with water during Sango's ceremony. In Trinidad, as in Haiti, Brazil and Jamaica, water is an important ritual element for the Yoruba tribe (Simpson 1970: 33). Not much water is needed during the rituals; just three drops on the ground during Sango's ritual would be enough to satisfy Sango and other Yoruba divinities.

ii. Osun and Divination in Trinidad: In Trinidad, Sango and Osun share some similarities. With the assurance of the divine power to protect and to fight for them, Sango devotees were keen to know the future. As mentioned earlier, Sango is the god of thunder and lightning, but his close association with other African divinities such as Osun gives him the ability to know and predict the future (Bascom 1944: 7). Also, as indicated earlier, Yoruba mythology states that Sango's best wife is Osun. Osun has sole ownership of the Sixteen Cowries of divination of Sango (Badejo 1995: 115). In Trinidad, religious divination and the use of cowries are accredited to Osun. Her priests guide and counsel the clients of Sango on matters of life and death. Frobenius, one of the priests of Osun, preferred to use kolanuts instead of the sixteen cowries, which had eight natural sections for divination (Simpson 1970: 96; Frobenius 1913: 1). Sango's message is revealed by counting the sixteen cowries or the kolanuts on the ground like dice. The revealed message is known by the number of kolanut pieces that are face-down or face-up. Different messages come with different incantations and only the priests have exclusive knowledge and interpretation of them.

In Trinidad, it is said that Sango lives in the sky and hurled thunderstones to the earth whenever he wanted to avenge those who had transgressed against him. He would hurl what the Yoruba people called *okuta Sango tabi edun ara* "thunderstones." Sango possesses a similar mission of vengeance as *Esu* 'devil' who also has the power to kill. But Sango seldom kills in the name of justice. Like Esu, Sango can only avenge when it is raining.

iii. Similarities in Sango and Osun: In Yoruba myths, Sango and Osun are very close relatives. Both shared a similar religious phenomenon which is connected with water: while Sango operates during the rainy season, Osun resides in the river. They are both considered as *orisa* 'god(dess)' by many Yoruba people. The Osun River gains more power and recognition with downpours of rain. No wonder, the Osun festival is celebrated during the rainy season in Nigeria, as is the Sango festival (Badejo 1995: 76).

iv. Sango's Taboos and Rules: Palmie stated that "in Cuba, the female deities Yemaya and Ochun, are described as the only oricha who will, at times, tolerate their powers to be put to amoral ends" (Palmie 2002: 165). Sango worship in Trinidad shared various practices with that of Osun. Sango's worship had governing rules for devotees. For example, worshippers must abstain from sexual intercourse three days before and three days after Sango's ceremony (Simpson 1970: 24). People are forbidden to smoke in the *palais* and from drinking alcoholic rum drinks. Participants are required to fast before the religious feast and before engaging in healing prayer sessions. As a sign of readiness, members are expected to bathe and put on clean clothing before going to a feast. Other ethical requirements for the participants are to avoid gambling, stealing and eating pork (ham) during the period.

v. Festivals and Ceremonies: Generally, religious festivals provide social and political opportunities for the African people to reconstruct their history and spirituality in the New World. For example, before the annual ceremony of Sango in Trinidad, leaders spend a lot of time collecting ritual materials for the occasion. They would collect general supplies like candles, bottles of olive oil, animals for sacrifices and groceries for the consumption of the devotees (Simpson 1970: 37). By going from house to house, they shared the joy of the season with their neighbors and the religious leadership got acquainted with the community. Other religious groups adopted the technique of parading in the streets, dancing in public and pouring libations for their divinities:

> The Spiritual Baptist religion in Trinidad shares many of the practices of African American spiritual and Pentecostal churches in the United States, including glossolalia, possession by the Holy Spirit, and ebullient and often extemporaneous singing, praising, and praying. The beliefs and practices .... Resemble those of the Orisha religion: for example, the libations of oil and water, the planting of flags for a particular spirit, and the recognition of the orisha as important spiritual forces (Houk 1995: 77).

This shows how one religion can benefit from the other. They both contribute to the social and spiritual growth of each other.

B. Osun in Jamaica

As we reach the last part of this book, we have to confess there are far less materials on Osun worship in Jamaica and Haiti. However, we find it necessary to say a few things about how Yoruba traditions impact on this part of the Island.

African religious cults are prominent in Cumina, Jamaica due to the presence of the people of Yoruba descent (Simpson 1970: 157). The majority of Jamaicans are black and their behavior and beliefs are similar to that of the Yoruba people. We can explain the reasons using the following example:

> The Jamaican negro was recruited entirely from West Africa. The Maroons probably came from Guinea (the rivers between the Gambia and Sierra Leone) and the Gold Coast: the Koromantis likewise from the Gold Coast; then there was a large importation from the Congo and Angola, the Calabar district (Mokos), the Niger Delta (Ibos), and some thousands from Lagos (Akus), Yoruba (Nagos), and Dahomé (Pōpōs) (Johnston 1969: 314).

It is very likely that those who came from Laos (Akus) and Yoruba (Nagos) revived the worship of Yoruba deities in Jamaica. African activities contributed to the growth of the Jamaican religious awareness and participation. Drumming, dancing, spirit possession and divination became common practices in Jamaica (Badejo 1995: 54, 157). These religious and social factors became common parts of the daily lives of Jamaicans.

The Santeria people remembered the significance of Osun and other Yoruba divinities in Jamaica. Life was difficult for the Yoruba descendants. At one time, the Yoruba were homesick and they wanted to go back to West Africa by any means.

> Still, after entering the British army and reaching Trinidad, Daaga and

the other Pōpōs and many of the kindred Yorubas of the regiment plotted to rise against their white masters, and after overpowering them to march back to Guinea by land! (Johnston 1969: 314).

As of 1955, there was an order that banned the African worship, saying "do not worship old African gods such as Legba, Damballa, Oogun, Obatala, Oshun, and Gede alongside the Catholic saints" (Simpson 1960: 89). But the threat did not eradicate the worship of African gods in Christianity.

Only a few Jamaicans have a deep knowledge of Osun as a diviner and healer but the rest of the people regularly attend their meetings (Badejo 1995: 13). They hear about Osun during the worship of other Yoruba divinities such as Orunmila, Ogun and Obatala. While Orunmila is widely known as the creator *ori inu* "human essence" in Jamaica, Osun is thought to be a giver of babies (Badejo 1995: 56). There is no way of dealing with one Yoruba god without mentioning the others.

Osun maintains her distinct image among the rest of Yoruba divinities. She is in-charge of waters, love, fertility and gold (Bjoring 1988: 107). Her spirit is readily available in support these areas of life.

One can make ritual for prosperity, beauty, love, and health through Osun and her Yoruba associates. This is a prescribed way to get things from Osun:

> Make a string of pearls with little bells on it, and buy a feathered fan that you spray with an expensive perfume. Place a bowl with honey on your altar and put into it five each on vanilla sticks, pumpkin pits, cloves, dashes of nutmeg, and cinnamon sticks. Stand in front of the altar, arm stretched out, and beg Oshun to fulfill your wishes. Make your entreaty in clear and unambiguous words (Owusu 2002: 28).

There is no record that those who followed these steps ever achieved anything in life. This is an individual consumer mentality of the Haitians.

C. Osun in Haiti

Haiti was a suitable place for African descendants. The vegetation, climate and topography of Haiti had always been suitable for the African religion. Materials for making herbal medicine, charms and sacrificial materials and ingredients could be easily found in Haiti because of it is a tropical region. Alfred Metraux states, "With the exception of a few desert regions, the whole of Haiti, from the coastal plains to the highest mountains, is occupied by the Africans" (Metraux 1960: 29). Haiti was thus a safe haven for the Africans immigrants to engage in their religious practices.

In sixteenth century Haiti, the Code Noir outlawed all non-Catholic worship. However, the Africans combined their traditional beliefs and practices with those of Catholicism (Bjorling 1988: 106). The reason why the majority of Catholic Church members contact the spirits of the African gods was that they did not feel totally secure just going to church services (Simpson 1970: 246). They needed extra security by using physical items that could bring them peace and security.

Slavery denied the African slaves the freedom of worship. By 1804, the majority of the slaves were still illiterates and their common language was Creole (Fisher 2004: x). Religious thoughts and beliefs were circulated by myths and rumors.

Just as it was on the other islands, traditional African religions had greatly influenced Haiti. An observer states that: "Anybody who has lived in [a] Haitian valley will recall those African rhythms which, wafted across by the wind, suddenly break the morning silence" (Metraux 1960: 33). African religions were not only practiced during the day, people also took time to celebrate the African divinities at night in Haiti. This was a strange form of religious practice to non-Africans living in Haiti.

Some scholars have attempted to play down the significance of African religion in Haiti. One such scholar stated that "they wish to prove that it is only a harmless... rural folklore with a touch of African background," that Haitians were mistaking for a real voodoo power (Metraux 1960: 59).

In contrast, other scholars including M. J. Herskovits, Alfred Metraux (Metraux 1972) and Harold Coulander, identified the contributions of African spirituality in Haiti. The growing interest of Haitians in voodoo was directly linked to the Africans. Almost every African on the island sought spiritual comfort and protection by the use of African power (Metraux 1960: 59). In Haiti, people freely employed voodoo for the purpose of gaining social, economic and political advantages over each other.

Haitians' religion of Voodoo is based on the African religion. There are statues and pictures of the Catholic saints, and rosaries standing side-by-side with the images of Yoruba gods. As a group of the Yoruba images, another African religious symbol of a major Voodoo spirit known as the *loa* were a common elements of worship. The *loa* is also called *zanger les spirit*, and *les mysteres* (Bjoring 1988: 106). These are the spirits of the African gods, especially the Yoruba ones such as Obatala, Ogun and Sango formed the major parts of the *loa*.

Voodoo spirituality is based on contacting the spirit of gods. These spirits are vengeance spirits. They fight the enemies of their worshippers. It was a religious custom of the Haitians to seek the assistance of their guardian spirits in all matters. It has been observed that frequently "the peasants bring sacrifices to the family guardian spirits, attend ceremonies in ... (temple) and respond to the calls of the drums" in order to achieve safety and prosperity (Metraux 1960: 59).

Osun worship was initially preserved as a part of the Haiti Catholicism, but when the slavery ended, Osun worship became an independent religious group among the people of African descent.

Osun worship is expressed more frequently in voodoo rituals and beliefs. Monaghan indicated that "Haitian Voudoun paintings show her as the Mater Dolorosa – the Catholic Virgin Mary who points to her pierced heart, through which several swords have cut" (Monaghan 2004: 193). Like other parts of the New World, Osun in Haiti became one of the Catholic saints. Her symbol of heart became an emblem of love that had gone through pains. The African worshippers could identify with the struggles, pains and hardships for which a pierced heart symbol stands for.

In Voodoo tradition, "for example, in the African feast cult, the Yoruba deity Oshun was associated with Saint Philomena" just like Yemanja with Saint Ann, Ogun with Saint Michael, and Osanyin with Saint Anthony (Bjorling 1988: 106). Osun shares her love freely with her ex-husbands, Erzulie and Shango. She enjoys freedom of association that people think of her as having many concubines. Heike Owosu says, "In Haiti, Oshun is worshiped as Erzulie, the divine concubine. None of her liaisons last very long. She was married for a short time to Shango, the god of fire, but since then has numerous affairs with other gods and men" (Owusu 2002: 25). It has been suggested that Shango may have been too volatile for Osun's tastes (Kaldera 2004: 141). She refused to be intimidated by male-dominated tradition or to be subjected to spouse abuse. Just as men had the freedom of association and relations, Osun became the role model for women in Haiti.

In Haitian Voodoo, Osun has favorite colors. In her association of Voodoo, "her colors are blue and pink" which apparently are the colors of the Virgin Mary (Monaghan 2004: 193). Osun is still associated with the most popular saints in the Catholic churches, therefore it impossible to forget her role in religious studies.

. Osun is also known and remembered for her sexual desire in Haiti religious worship. Osun is known well, for "her cult was characterized by the Europeans as some unspecified 'obscene worship'" (Littlewood 1993: 140). Karen Tate explained that Osun was faithful to her mythological ex-husbands, by saying "while monogamy might not be Oshun's forte, she is considered loyal, refusing to have her behavior defined by social mores" (Tate 2006: 132). Hence Osun became a model of faithfulness in marriage for most of her worshippers.

Osun likes sculpture and painting. Fine arts are expressions of love and passion in religious studies (Owusu 2002: 27). Jewels are rich symbols of Osun worshippers that keep the memory of Osun divinity alive.

Osun is also a healer. She loves life and she wants her devotees to enjoy divine healing and divine health. It is written that "she heals the sick over the cool waters that also belong within her realm" (Owusu 2002: 25-27). No wonder people on the both sides of the Atlantic Ocean still recognize the lordship of Osun.

1. Haiti Syncreticism

Osun is known in Haiti as "coquettish Erzulie-Freda-Dahomey" (Monaghan 2004: 192). Osun was renamed to suit the new setting and new people that wanted to connect to the water goddess.

Scholars agreed in their observations that African and Western religions complemented each other in Haiti. After all, it was noted that "having co-existed for two centuries, Catholicism and African cults are finally merged into [a] conception of a universe…" in Haiti's setting (Metraux 1960: 59). The African religion adopted some practical ideas from Catholicism. For instance, firstly, in organizational structures and administration, the African religion has learned from Catholicism to be orderly. Secondly, the African groups started paying more attention to hygiene in preparation for their services.

Furthermore, it is noted that "usually, most services to African gods are introduced by thanksgiving" a practice that is not common in Yorubaland. These invocations and processional hymns can be traced back to Christian influences (Metraux 1960: 59).

2. Religious Meetings - Spontaneous Prayers

African religious meetings in Haiti became daily, weekly and monthly ceremonies (Metraux 1960: 60). African religious groups were opened to anybody to join. In Yorubaland, most people celebrate divinities in exclusive settings, e.g. sacred forest, shrines. In Haiti, Catholic Christians meet weekly and sometimes daily, for mass and every member of the public is welcome to attend. In like manner, Africans in Haiti now erect shrines outside their homes and build a canopy for people to join them in service (Metraux 1960: 59).

In order to encourage participation, African gods are said to be quicker in responding to people's prayers than Catholic saints. Africans involved in magic encourage quick fixes for their problems. The names of their gods have the power to perform magic whenever they are invoked (Metraux 1960: 60).

Scholars have noted that the Haitian African deities vary in popularity. There are those "which everybody has always known and respected, there exist many whose fame is recent and local and who are worshipped by only a small group" (Metraux 1960: 60). The less significant African religions are those that have fewer followers, due to the exclusive membership policy and because they did not meet the general needs of the people.

In Haiti, the less recognized deities' shrines are covered in pictures and candles and only a few people pay attention to them and participate in their worship services. One of the reasons is that African divinities are too specialized in various aspects of human life and, if one does not need them, one has no cause to attend their services.

African shrines are available to anybody who may be interested in paying homage to the African divinities. A shrine may have a couple of visitors in a month (Metraux 1960: 60). The Yoruba pray everywhere and at any time to their divinities. They neither need a priest nor cathedral to pray. Prayers rendered at the shrines are as effective as the ones offered elsewhere.

3. African Religious Music

Music is a form of prayer in African religion. It is full of memories and histories of the religion (Olatunji: 69-86). These people sing just as Catholic church members chant prayers to Mary, Peter and the rest of the respectable saints (Metraux 1960: 60). Africans use songs to awaken the spirits of the divinities and their ancestors to attend to the prayers (Olajubu 1970: 31-51). The difference between them and Catholics is that African music and songs are often very loud and conducted in unison. African music attracts different kinds of people to their services. It was reported that, "they are an odd crowd, almost impossible to count...", and they gather spontaneously on hearing the music, drum and song. People come up with creative songs and musical instruments in worshipping African divinities (Metraux 1960: 60). They saw no harm in dancing all night in honor of their gods and yet going to Mass in the Catholic Church the next day (Metraux 1960: 56).

This thesis strongly agrees with Rebecca Sophia Sargent's statement that Osun is an important goddess in Caribbean religion such as Voudoun, Candoble, Santeria, and Shango worship (Sargent 2003: 191). Some of the myths that survived in the Old and the New Worlds helped in retaining the memories of Osun worship. Her memories and significances in the African and African-Americans are preserved in symbols and images of myths.

To avoid persecution from their masters, African slaves in the New World initially refrained from celebrating their African-originated religion openly. The African slaves had to conceal their religious activities from their masters. In Brazil, for instance, "there is no doubt that under the pretext of Catholic festivity, they were really celebrating African divinities" (Verger 1976: 471). People of the Africa diaspora had vivid recollections of their home-based religions, but because of slavery they had to practice their faith in secret. But, after some time, they received government support in practicing their religion.

Today, Yoruba deities such as Osun co-exists side-by-side with Christianity. To prove the extent of African religion in the New World, internet sites are full of 'made-in-America' images of Osun. Religious practices can travel beyond their original boundary without scriptures as we have seen with Osun in the New World. In a hostile environment during slavery, African religion kept its history and practice alive in the New World. Merlin Hernandez expressed the same sentiments:

> A spirit is not something [that] has a temporal existence. A spirit is an essence, and that essence in India will be given a name; that essence in Africa will be given a name; that essence in Native America will be given a name. And whether you have Oshun in Yoruba.., it's the same essence (Houk 1995: 114).

Osun worship, in particular, was unstoppable in Cuba, Brazil, Trinidad, Jamaica and Haiti. Her history is going through a lot of reconstruction on African-American websites. How did it happen? Here are some common denominators.

African religion, in general, finds common ground in different parts of the world. Considering the long years of separation of Africans from their homeland, the slave trade, the abolition of slavery and relocation of ex-slaves, African religious history survived all ordeals. Individuals who returned to Africa shared with others the stories of what the lifestyle overseas had in common with life in Africa. One of the things the returned ex-slaves did was to change their names to more indigenous names. It was reported in Nigeria that "from the 1880s onwards, the Lagos newspapers were flooded with notices of people who had Brazilian or English names and were changing them to African names" (Verger 1985: 34). It was, however, a deliberate action on the parts of the returnees to reintegrate into the local setting of African culture and people.

Africans and the African descendants in the world usually enjoyed a sense of brotherhood whenever they met each other, especially in a religious context. In the preface to his 1993 work, *The African*, Harold Courlander explained that religion is one of the strong common ties that united the Africans and Black African-Americans together as one. He said that religious beliefs give them "a sense of relationship to the world around them and to the unseen but living forces of the universe" (Matibag 1996: 11).

In this work, so far, we found that Osun was not a mere religious figure in the Yoruba religion but she became a prominent religious figure among the male-dominated deities. Sango, a prominent divinity of the Yoruba, is on the same level of popularity with Osun in worship. Just like Sango, Osun had followers from different parts of African countries (Simpson 1970: 17; Bascom, II. 1944: 29). As early as 1852, the Sango cult, like many other African religions, had fully developed into a religious movement in Trinidad (Simpson 1970: 13). It was noted that one Charles W. Day "was often annoyed by the drumming and dancing of plantation workers" who jubilantly observed the Sango festival (Simpson 1970: 13). We did not come across any case where such people were annoyed about the Osun celebration.

As in Yorubaland, "Osun" became a common prefix in the names of some Yoruba descendants in the New World. Yoruba names often reinforce the memories of the African divinities around the world. African surnames always reflect the family's religious affiliations (Warner-Lewis 1999: 20-21). These names are symbolical and historical.

Most features of Yoruba religion such as offering sacrifice, ritual, drumming and dancing happened frequently in the New World. The "cosmological, theological, ceremonial, magical and medical aspects" of Yoruba religious activities are common in the New World (Badejo 1995: 54). Africans are one of the most cultured groups in the New World (Simpson 1970: 11). Osun was an active divinity on the other side of the Atlantic Ocean (Badejo 1995: 43, 56). Most of the Sango worshippers' regularly organized parties for the children of Sango (Simpson 1970: 45). Religious ceremonies were conducted in a spirit of thanksgiving to all African divinities. One member said, "when you feed the children, you feed the saints" (Badejo 1995: 13).

The European influences and reinterpretations of the African religious elements became clearer as they were allowed into the Catholic churches (Simpson 1970: 142). They freely used magic books and spells in the new setting (Simpson 1970: 105). They also adopted the use of candles, crosses, crucifixes and incense like the Catholics. Africans were not ashamed to adopt European-influenced religions and cultures (Simpson 1970: 105). To them, culture was dynamic therefore it could be adjusted to suit any historical setting (Bascom and Herskovits 1959: 2).

Santeria was born on the other side of the Atlantic. Harry Lefever argues that Santeria is a "textual" religion from which people could rewrite the biography, the history and the social contexts of its adherents. This study is a representation of how African religions have been retained in the Old and the New Worlds, by focusing on Osun myths. Santeria, a new age religious movement, grew out of African religions, most especially the

Yoruba religion. Santeria became a developing religion in Cuba from the sixteenth to the nineteenth centuries. As syncretism of Yoruba religions, Roman Catholicism and French spiritism, Santeria became established in different parts of the New World (Okpewho, Davies, Mazuri 1999: 379-380).

James Houk states that, "The syncretism of Catholic saints and African gods- *orisha, voodoo* or others – is one of the more salient and prevalent characteristics of African-derived religions in the New World" (Houk 1995: 180). Syncretism could be defined as the coming together of African divinities and Christianity in forms, images and worship; the result gave birth to Santeria in which the worshippers practice blood sacrifice, spirit possession, ancestor worship and herbal healing (Houk 1995: 76). Osun became a prominent figure in it. She gained the religious recognition of the Catholic saints. Priests and popes recognized her divinity. Hence, African religions in the New World have influenced the papacy to accept a non-western divinity into their lists of saints. As a saint in Santeria, Osun gives people supernatural power over the challenges of life, a mediator between God and the people.

In the consumer age, Osun is making her way into the minds of children of all ages and races. Osun can help teenage girls make direct contact with their inner Goddess energy (Marie-Jeanne 2002: 131). She can assist anybody in mediations, visualizations and other spiritual exercises.

8
Osun Worship and Mythological Studies

The hypothesis of this book is to describe the Osun worship and its spread in the New World. From the the beginning of our research, we assumed that this would be a treatment of the historical development of a Yoruba goddess in the developed world. We did not know better at the time. Now we can say that the task is accomplished only through the retelling of Yoruba myths. In light of this investigation, we come to the conclusion that Osun of Osogbo is the same Ochun of Cuba, Brazil, Trinidad, Jamaica and Haiti. She is a recognized goddess in the Old and the New World and Osun is a canonized saint of the Catholic Church. Her fame has gone beyond anybody's expectation. Osun therefore serves as an example of the development and growth of African religion in the twenty-first century. One can say that African religion is not just "African" any more but now it is now an intercontinental religion.

In the first chapter it is obvious that the history of African religious could be treated by focusing on the importance of oral tradition as a form of religious scripture. We demonstrated the use of descriptive mythological methodology as an appropriate way of understanding the Yoruba religion.

Chapters two and three explored the history of Osun in Osogbo. Here we demonstrated that religious figures and sacred sites retain the history of religion and information that forms the religious lifestyles of the people. It was found that, in order to understand the Yoruba frame of thought, one has to study their history through religious festivals. We focused strictly on studying the historical figures and elements in the Osun festival. We discovered that festivals are held annually in order to please the spirit of Osun and for the followers to remember their historical origins. All leaders involved in Osun rituals had a mandate to obey their ancestor to the letter in the way they carried out their responsibilities. Religious leaders were always available to guide the rest of the participants. This practice continued from one generation to another to avoid gaps in knowledge and loss of memories.

The chapters four, five, six and seven explained the spread and the continuation of Osun in the New World. Cuba, Brazil, Trinidad, Jamaica and Haiti were highlighted, to argue that Osun worship is flourishing due to the retelling of her myths and those of other African divinities. Without sending delegates and without sharing any information on how Osun should be honored and worshipped, many of their practices are similar to that which exists in Osogbo today. I discovered that after many generations of separation of the Yoruba people on both sides of the Atlantic, the religious elements still guide their devotion to Osun.

Africans in the Americas gave birth to a new religion known as Santeria. The continuation and the spread of African religion and culture is everywhere, even in Europe, Asia and the Middle East. One can see African influences in dressing, worship, food and commerce in America, Asia and Europe. African religion and worldview basically form a part of human experience.

An African religious festival in Osogbo is a very dynamic annual religious event which displays a phenomelogical and existential idea of religion. In learning about this festival, one could not but focus on the religious significance as a way of gaining a deep understanding of its relevance to the people. It is a religious festival that shows the cosmological, sociological, political and historical dimension of religion. By comparing various practices and interpretations of Osun worship, we are able to reconstruct its history and link it to its survival in the Americas. Osun worship in Osogbo and in the New World is influencing the religious and political structures of the place it found itself (Badejo 1995: 48). Festival, ritual, sacrifice and drama are constant reminders of the Yoruba worldview. Religious worship was focused on by using African myths in the reconstructing the history of Osun.

Here are some of the challenges we encountered in our research. African religious thought is hidden in myths, folktales, riddles, stories and superstitions. For instance, folktales as elements of fiction are not dogma or history per se. Moral issues and ethics are demonstrated in the lives of the past leaders. These people had an influence on the definition of communal moral ethics that guarded the religious elements, especially during Yoruba festivals. Today, globalization allows the kings and chiefs to travel overseas anytime without providing adequate supervisions for the cultural and traditional of their subjects.

In this book, we discover how significant myth is in understanding and preserving of a Yoruba God in a new environment. The interest of media, religion and culture is apparent in this topic too. We notice that there is a competition among the leadership of recognition and financial support. In this work we see how the Yoruba people express themselves in both good and bad times. We see an evolution of their religion in a new religious organization and new geographical setting. The New World is a larger context and through immigration it is becoming a broader culture. In this case, we notice spiritual overlaps with intuition, inspiration, illumination and creativity in religious worship.

As we shall explain in the next chapter, myth theorists such as Levi-Strauss, Ferdinand de Saussure, Carl G. Jung, Mircea Eliade, and Rudolf Bultmann, although they were not specialists in the Yoruba religion, their works on the theories of myth are helpful in scholarship. Irving Hexham also gives a useful definition of myth that is similar to the one we are going to apply in this study. He defines myth as "a type of narrative which seeks to express in imaginative form a belief about man, the world, and/or GOD or gods which cannot adequately be expressed in simple PROPOSITIONS" (Hexham 1993: 153). The use of gender in Hexham's definition is all-inclusive, for myth could be a narrative about everybody and everything in any part of the world.

Another definition of myth is given by Eric Csapo, who says:

> Myths are the embodiment of dogma; they are usually often associated with theology and ritual. Their main characters are not usually human beings, but they often have human attributes; they are animals, deities, or culture heroes, whose actions are set in an earlier world such as the sky or underworld (Csapo 2005: 4).

This definition tells us about the contents of myths: dogma, theology and ritual. It even informs us about the attributes of the actors involved in a myth. However, it is not clear to us whether myth leads to formation of religious dogma, or that the dogmas created myths in order to keep the community doctrine alive.

As we have read, Yoruba myths have various characters which include deities, human beings, heroes, heroines, animals and nature. The contents and variants of these myths vary from one community to another. However, there are similar recurring motifs in myths seen in the various versions of the story of the creation of the world and of the origin of mankind, in the many stories explaining the meaning of death, the moon, the rainbow, lightning and thunder, and in the many stories of animals. Myths are full of humor, wit, cruelty, and anguish; their repetitive elements make them entertaining while explaining fundamental concerns, beliefs and desires.

Myths provide and preserve useful information about the people, culture and religion. Ben-Amos says "actually, the idea that tales and songs, proverbs and riddles follow communicable structural principles is a theoretical statement about the nature of activity and performance" when it comes to arts and entertainments (Ben-Amos: 18). Myth has linguistic lines that make it form a story for the community. It usually supports the existing rites and rituals of the community. In the Yoruba religion as in other African religions, myth is often confused with tale, legend, folklore or mere story, "this implies no JUDGEMENT on the TRUTH of the story" (Hexham 1993: 153). The truth of the matter is that a true and historical story can become a myth. Eric Csapo makes a clear distinction between myths and legends, "legends are often secular rather than sacred, and their principal characters are human. They tell of migrations, wars, and victories, deeds of the past heroes, chiefs, and kings, and the succession in ruling dynasties" (Csapo 2005: 4). Thus, Csapo distinguishes legend from myth, for myth is concerned with the sacred as well as the secular. They all reveal something significance to people in another cultural and religious context.

Both myth and legend fall under the same classification as the oral narrative in Yoruba religious studies. Legend is often staged as story for entertainment. Legend could become a myth as the community verifies the authenticity and credibility of its contents. Tale, legend, folklore and story have differences in nature, quality, length, actor, and genre.

Another term that is often confused with myth is illusion in Yoruba religious studies. The word 'myth' and 'illusion' are synonymous for some, but the term 'myth' is more strongly connected to the historical event that inspired the story than to an illusion. Myth also has ritual elements, structural and functional purposes that illusion does not have in the community (Okpewho: vii). Myth unites people, community and religion as one, although all those involved may not agree completely with the majority's interpretations. However, we can talk of the Yoruba community myths as a unified force behind their culture and religion.

Myth is a sacred tale that commands people's awe as the narrators relate it to their audience (Okpewho: ix). Myth is a creative and logical way for sustaining the cultural values of every generation (Okpewho ix). The text and context of myth appeal to human empathy and function as more than entertainment or ritual. Myth is meaningful as a religious term (Gilkey 1970: 101-137). Many myths effect changes in the lives, cultures and religious beliefs of people around the world.

Monica Wilson (1908-82), a leading African historian and anthropologist, who taught at Rhodes University and the University of Cape Town, noticed the different usage of the term myth. She states: "the anthropologist uses the term to mean an account of past events *told as fact*, but which can be shown to be partly fictitious, or at least a grave distortion of historical fact" (Monica Wilson, 1). She worked with the definition in her works *Good Company* (1951), *Rituals of Kinship* 1957), *Communual Ritual* (1959), and *For Men and Elders* (1977).

Irving Hexham (1943-), a professor in the Department of Religious Studies at the University of Calgary, pointed out that "myth has been held to be a truer or deeper version of REALITY than SECULAR HISTORY, realistic description or scientific explanations" by some scholars (Hexham 1993: 153). Others believe that myth is a combination of fiction and distorted historical events. Whichever the case, the community is often left with the responsibility of keeping the myth intact as oral narratives for the future generation. For the community, "myths purport to *explain* existing relations in terms of history. They also provide a *moral basis* for a social system. They imply, if they do not state specifically, that a given system is right and just" (Monica Wilson: 1). Myth serves vital purposes in different communities and cultures.

Myth influences the decisions of the Yoruba kingdoms. Myth serves an important role in sustaining religious beliefs, social interpersonal relationships and in keeping cultural institutions alive. To support this claim Monica Wilson states that "in all societies stories are told which justify the existing political system" (Monica Wilson 1). On the pragmatic level, it seems that myth works like advertisement slogan in the minds of the people. This kind of myth is what is called the "settlers myth" (Monica Wilson 3). This assumption supports traditional beliefs of the local community.

The "true" nature of myth varies from one society to another. But they all agree on the tradition that myth is neither the first nor the last word in the history of a community, for they appear almost unwanted and unexpected in. Some myths are common across the borders and other myths are not popular among people. Some myths are simple stories and others are full of mysteries and scary characters. The images and roles of different characters in myths contribute to their sustainability. Some myths are for mere poetical lines and others for political gains in the community. Most are told for entertainment and utilized as teaching aids for the community. All myths have another thing in common, they appeal to people's imaginations. Human beings have curious minds that are always searching for meaning behind myth. Curiosity and imagination contribute to the life of myths.

All myths also have cognitive features in common, such as generic names and genres. When they come in either written or spoken form they are called oral narratives. Another common feature of myths is that they all allow room for individual commentaries, thought context, and varied content and audience. For this reason, similar or even identical myths have had very different effects.

Myths have expressive features in common. Each has an opening and closing formula, style, content and structure. These expressive features make it easier to classify myth as a fiction or fact in the life of the community. As we study the significance of names in myths, one could trace the origin of such myth based on its genres. Myth has social features and some myths share same contents and expressions in common. Myth can be for mere entertainment, for persuasion or to generate a debate. Myth is rooted in cultural thought, language, and experience. It is important for students of religion to understand the original language of the people they are studying in other not to misinterpret its contents. Different forms of myths reflect distinctions of cultural conception, social structure and religion of the people.

Although "critics of myth argue that it tends to open the door to IRRATIONALISM" some communities still find solace in myth (Hexham 1993: 153). Myth serves different functions to different people depending on the contents of the myth and the context of the people. Some myths are basically for religious purposes from which people actually learn more about their religious past. Other myths are mainly tales in which the protagonists happen to bear the names of the gods and ancestors. Such myths have historical, rather than religious function (Beier: xvi). There are other myths which "were invented by the spiritual leaders to provide a precedent, with the help of which the priest can advise his client on the right course of action to take" (Beier: xiv).

According to psychoanalytical works, dreams and experiences formed the major contents of myths (Okpewho, 8-9). For the psychoanalysts, myths are primordial symbols or *archetypes* (otherwise called *mythologems*) for the primitive mind (Okpewho 11-12). According to Freud and Jung, the primitive mind precedes the civilized thinking era. They insist that the primitive mind did not invent myth, but that they experienced it firsthand at a particular time and place (Okpewho 12). Hence, the sophistication of myth determines the basis of cultural thought and level of intelligence of people in a community. One needs to pay attention to the evidence of developmental stages of cultural myth.

It has been observed that "myths are highly selective. Certain historical events are picked out and exaggerated, perhaps sometimes even invented. And the selection of course, is not haphazard, for the myths always, in some measure, reflect the existing social structure; but they are also potent forces for stability or change; they help to maintain an existing social structure or create a new one" (Monica Wilson, 6). There are creative elements in myth which make them memorable in nature (Okpewho ix). One of the criteria in preservation of myth is that it must have a verbal and literary expressive quality that appeal to people of different gender, age, and culture. Myth come in different styles and versions, and a myth can be heard repeatedly in a variety of forms and settings. All have in common the merit of literature that can be enjoyed by the audience.

Working with myths is not a simple task in Yoruba religious studies. Myths come in pieces. Bringing the myths together in narratives requires creativity. Ben Amos rightly noted that "actually, the idea that tales and songs, proverbs and riddles follow communicable structural principles is a theoretical statement about the nature of creativity and performance" (Ben-Amos 18). Richard Mercer Dorson (1972), William Russell Bascom (1969, 1975), Saburi O. Biobaku (1973), Isidore Okpewho (1983, 1992), Graham Furness (1995) and Jan Vansina (2006) had successfully used mythological method in their works.

The functions of myths are numerous as we have seen in this work. In the Yoruba community, for instance, myths explain how some people and animals are from above and others are from below. Myths portray the divinities as human beings and as if these beings have historial characters. They attempt to explain the existence of animal, place or thing. In a way, myths help in bringing a community together. They are preserved and retold during ritual and by that give a community a common view of world. Myths provide, sustain and protect the moral values of a community. They provide paths that make people conscious of the world. We observed that myths have elements of rumor that function as motivators for improving human conduct. Myths bridge the intergenerational gaps that exist between old and new generations in a community. They can be so amusing in illustrating the beliefs and worldview of people. Last but not the least myths have the potential of transforming individual or community by leading them into phenomena spiritual experience.

As it has been said, each myth "provides the means by which man can move towards" wholeness and develop a communion with divinities (Father F. T. Sillent, 9). Myths encourage people to develop positive and creative relationships with fellow men and their divinities. Myths have implications for history and poetry, function and art, structure and sensibility because myths influence them all (Okpewho: vii). Myths have connections to the works of arts (Okpewho: ix). They preserve the stories behind the arts.

Freud taught that folktales are derived from the interaction between daydreams and ardent desires nurtured in the mind of people in the community (Okpewho, 10). Eric Csapo indicates that "folktales may be set in any time and any place, and in this sense they are almost timeless and placeless" (Csapo 2005: 4). Unlike folktales, the contents of myths are located in time and space of 'long time ago' or 'once upon a time'. We need to point out that the two phrases above are commonly used in retelling the Yoruba myths.

As in this book, myths should be taken seriously and they should be appreciated in understanding the Yoruba people, religion and culture that are located in different parts of the world. In this case, myths are important in understanding the Yoruba worship of Osun in the Old and the New Worlds. Myths therefore connect the Yoruba people of Nigeria with their descendants in the New World.

The best way to study a Yoruba religion is to have a good skill of Yoruba language, cultural and historical knowledge of the people. We would recommend that any individual who wanted to study the Yoruba people and their religion should spend years around them so as to grasp the people's thinking pattern. In addition one should seek to get all documented materials on the people and their religion. Jan G. Platvoet acknowledged the difficulty of accessing information on the Yoruba oral literature when he said, "though much of their histories [are] and will forever remain unknown, and the little we know is often obtained by very fallible means, yet we have sufficient data to establish with some confidence a number of categories of Yoruba religions as historical" (Paltvoet 1996: 47). One has to squeeze out information from people who are familiar with the religion.

The Yoruba religious materials that are available need to be substantiated by a number of other useful source materials. Oral literature, where available, are retained and relayed in parts. Fascinating knowledge is hidden in them, if they are carefully put together to form a storyline (Bascom 1981:66-67). Bascom writes, "verbal art is composed and transmitted verbally, while literature is composed in writing and transmitted in writing;" and what scholars need to do is to fix the puzzles to get accurate knowledge of the religion (Bascom 1981: 71). Certainly, it is hard for those who are not familiar with oral literature to quickly understand the details of such fragmented materials.

Religious studies often rely heavily on past events to explain current religious practices in any given oral society. Without dates and eyewitness documentation, it is a challenging task to link the historical past with present developments in oral religious settings (Bascom

1981: 79). Doing research without written documents is becoming even more difficult nowadays when the "loss of memory does occur" and as migration and immigration are common phenomena in Yoruba cities (Bascom 1967: 51). People's interest in myths, folklore and legends is being traded for technological advancements and innovations. A number of priests, healers and parents who knew the details of oral literature regularly recite them to their children (Awolalu 1996: 69; Olajubu 1970). Yoruba music and drama regularly feature myths and tales in their works (Matibag 1996: 77).

Most of the stories associated with Osun practices are preserved orally in both sides of the Atlantic. Oral tradition and practice constantly revive people's thought of gods and goddesses. *Itan* "stories," *owe* "proverbs", *ijala* "hunters' dirges," *ewi* "praise-poetry," *ofo* incantations," *aloo* "riddles and jokes," enrich the study of the Yoruba religion. Drumming, music and songs contribute to the structures of the Yoruba religion. These sources are educational to the Yoruba people.

John Roberts, one of the contributing authors in the *African Origins and New World Identities*, argues that African oral narratives, accompanied by drums and dancing, contribute to the reconstruction of African history of religion (Okpewho, Boyce Davis, and Mazrui: xix). It has been rightly said by another scholar that:

> It is impossible to study any history anywhere if one is not thoroughly acquainted with the culture of the people whose past it is, and if one cannot understand the sources in the original languages in which they are spoken. This is obvious but, in regard to the study of oral traditions, this rule has been neglected so often that it must be stated again (Bascom 1967: 43).

In an attempt to understand the Yoruba myths, Sandra Greene emphasizes the need to cover other areas that are non-religious. She argued that in order not to miss the clear picture of religious developments, we need to pay attention to "the dynamic and non-doctrinaire characters of African religious practices as well as the centrality of the history of politics and power" in Africa (Greene 1996: 126). It is easy for religious studies to overlook religious implications of myths in festival on international developments. Religious festival is an occasion where spiritual and government leaders meet with the community members in celebrating a divinity. The religious and cultural thoughts are knitted together in preserving and promoting their spiritual beliefs. Spiritual leaders are more involved in planning and carrying out religious festivals than the secular community leaders. In a way, religious festivals provide the community the opportunities to revisit the myths of their beliefs. Myths become meaningful when studied in the context of a festival. Myths often elaborate the Yoruba *owe* (proverbs), *ijala* (hunters' songs), *alo* (riddles) and *efe* (jokes). They are reliable oral literature for entertainments and in understanding the moral and ethical beliefs of a community. Indirectly, the re-telling of myths during a festival renews people's interest in believing the divinities.

Due to the fact that spiritual leaders are the major organizers of festivals, scholars value their assistance in understanding myths. Benjamin C. Ray says that "the study of African religions is generally a mutual understanding between scholars and indigenous priests and priestesses" (Ray 2000: 78). This does not make the job simple, for there are other challenges in the way of a student of religion in understanding a divinity, a myth, and its interpretation.

Here are various challenges one faces in studying a Yoruba myths. Firstly, the majority of the Yoruba oral literature is not available in print. One anthropologist lamented that "no histories of these religions could be produced because they had no texts" (Platvoet 1992, 1996:

115). Yoruba myths are retained mainly in people's minds, in cultural and religious practices. On a daily basis, Yoruba priests recollect parts of the myths in the form of incantations as they meet with the believers (Awolalu 1996: 69; Olajubu 1970). The Yoruba religion has not got to the same documentation stage as the Western and Eastern religions, where religious materials had become scriptures (Ojo 1969: 12). In those traditions such as Hinduism, Buddhism, Judaism, Christianity and Islam, it is easier to compare scriptures with scriptures and to work with the original languages of the texts than working with oral literature.

The second concern when working with oral literature in Yorubaland is that public museums in Nigeria have been exclusively devoted to the collections that support traditional cultures and not religious materials (Ojo 1969:12). Until 1960, anthropologists' works generally directed their efforts mainly on issues that benefited the European colonial administrators (Platvoet 1992, 1996: 110). Anthropologists studied the actual practice and lifestyle of the Yoruba people in order to help the colonial staff in governing the Yoruba people effectively (Platvoet 1992, 1996: 115; Ogot, 1970: 182-183; Ranger and Kimambo 1972: 2-3, 9).

The third challenge one faces in working with the Yoruba oral literature is the climatic and human factors on the available items. The West African communities regularly experienced floods, humidity and dry weather which destroyed the majority of materials that were available for a research. For instance, Ojo described what he saw of "rattles and anklets used in Osun cult… one has broken away to reveal the iron loop on which the clapper is hooked" (Ojo 1969: 12). Woodcarved images associated with the Osun festival and other divinities in Yorubaland were rotten from the termites' bites (Ojo 1979: 334). The leftover materials that are available are being looted by local people and being sold to foreigners. Ulli Beier recounted his experience in Nigeria by stating,

> During the years 1900 to 1966 when I was able to keep in close touch with all the important shrines in the Oshogbo area, I have not come across a case of a single voluntary sale. But numerous objects were stolen. Even when the museum or police were able to retrieve the objects, however, there was no efficient machinery to deal with the thieves (Beier 1972: 32).

The other groups of people who have sabotaged Yoruba works of arts are the converts to Christianity and Islam (Peel 1967: 292-306). It started with a widespread religious change in Yorubaland and which continues up till now. Ulli Beier also wrote,

> Travelling in Western State recently I discovered with horror that some Christian churches still collect traditional Yoruba art objects (labeled by them as 'idols') from converts and that these are burnt annually. Apparently, present day legislation renders the Department of Antiquities powerless to act in such a case (Beier 1972: 33).

Such religious articles were mainly individual and personal collections that were no longer needed by the people for worship. As the owners converted to Christianity or Islam, they had to burn their traditional religious materials for they had no need of them anymore (Peel 1967: 292-306). The so-called fetish materials were set on fire to show the converts' genuine determination to follow their newfound faith. It is an act of holiness to get rid of these so called "demonic" items.

These are just a few of the challenges facing the students and scholars who have interest in studying Yoruba myths. One has to look for different ways to secure oral literature. Here are the surviving elements of the Yoruba religion: myths and religious.

Generally speaking, Yoruba religious festivals keep parts of the myths alive. The religious leaders have been very helpful in maintaining the credibility and the standard of worship in their different communities. The leaders are the custodians of the religious materials for the community. These spiritual leaders have the responsibility of transmitting such information to their successors.

A common way of collecting information on oral religion is by contacting and contracting informants. One has to pay for their services either in cash or in kind. The informants' job is more important than just tour-guides. Generally, these local people have a better understanding of the religious activities and beliefs of their people. In most cases, these religious tour-guides are born and bred in the community, therefore they know a lot about the topic. Whenever specialist help is needed, informants can recommend and take the researchers to priests.

Myths are sacred and the priests have knowledge of most of them. Informants are a good source for myths, though some of them do not have enough materials to work with for a big project. Priests usually have more accurate information on oral materials than ordinary members of a community. But one has to go through an informant to contact reputable priests who are knowledgeable about different areas of oral narratives. Local priests are primary custodians of sacred materials. Benjamin Ray emphasized the importance of consulting local priests for academic research (Ray 2000: xiii). In the Yoruba community, local priests are called *babalawo,* "herbalists." They are well versed in poetry known as *ofo* (incantations) which are full of Yoruba myths. Incantations contain a lot of information regarding the story behind each event in the community. Myths empower ritual prescriptions for effective healing and cure of diseases (Ray 2000: 78). A *babalawo* is one of the most skillful narrators of Yoruba myths and history. Scholars often seek their assistance for specific information on religious and historical subjects.

Once contact has been established between a researcher and an informant, it is the responsibility of the scholar to ask the right questions. It is the task of the researcher to collect, to compile and to rightly create and outline the collected information to substantiate one's thesis. It is required that one should note the names, addresses, dates and times of contact for future reference (Oruka 1983: 388). Such documented religious thought must be verified with other sources (Bascom 1981: 79). The credibility of informants and priests is vital when recollecting, recording and forming the right sequences of the history of traditional religion (Bascom 1967: 47).

Due to the different nature of the informants involved in collecting research data, one has to verify its authenticity. One piece of information could mislead a researcher to make an erroneous interpretation and conclusion that may undermine an entire work. Based on misleading information that Deidre L. Badejo received, she concluded that the Osun festival is an annual religious drama. Badejo said,

> Osun festival and its oral literature provide the context, content, meaning, and symbolism that mirror the complexities of sacred and secular dramatic art. The interplay between the divinities is annually remembered in [the] Osun festival. The annual ritual imprisonment of Obatala at Osogbo is a dramatic time when there is no spoken dialogue but singing accompanies the performance (Clark 1996: 119).

Most of the words used in these statements indicate to us that Badejo saw the Osun festival as a mere cultural drama and performance. Badejo interpreted the drumming, singing, and dancing as entertainment rather than religious activities that had religious meaning (Badejo 1996: 135). As we shall argue, the Osun festival is not orchestrated for secular entertainment but is rather a form of a spiritual renewal festival (Beier 1977: 13). Yoruba religious festivals do not fit in a stage-play. Too much dependence on informants in researching a religion could be misleading (Okpewho 1980: 11). Paul Stoller was also a victim of misinformation. In his research, some important religious information was purposefully concealed from him (Bourdillon 1996: 142).

Another means of securing information on the history of African religion is through curators. Scholars can use the wide collections in museums as a starting point for researching projects. In Yorubaland, the museums' collection processes have been criticized for being partial, because "public museums in Nigeria have so far been exclusively devoted to the preservation of traditional cultures" (Ojo 1969: 12). Government officials pay little attention to the collection of religious materials. Until 1960, the Yoruba religious collections had exclusively focused on collecting works of art.

Curators know different versions of myths surrounding particular objects in their centers. Depending on who one met on duty, each curator has a different interpretation for the same object. It is the responsibility of scholars to decide which one to take seriously. Religious items in a museum speak volumes on the history of the Yoruba religion but their messages can only be heard through voices of the curators (MacGaffey 2000: 228).

Yoruba sculptures are considered to be sacred objects and are symbols of certain historical events of the community. Yoruba arts "are frequently mythical or supernatural" and create fear in the mind of curators which leads them to tell the truth about the items under their care (Bascom 1967: 1). The curator has both a moral obligation to educate their visitors that religious objects and sites serve as reminders of the past for the community (Warner-Lewis 1999: 22).

For instance, significant interest was generated in Yoruba objects in 1912 when Leo Frobenius made an archeological discovery of the Ife bronzes. These bronzes revealed the meticulous works of art and religious past of the Ife people, the cradle of all Yoruba (Bascom 1967:1). Since then, the Ife bronzes have generated academic discussions on the Yoruba people (Bascom 1967: 7). Wole Soyinka, a Nobel Prize winner, also concluded that Yoruba culture is rich in myths and religious symbols (Deidre 1995: 117). However, curators change from time to time and their knowledge of the items are very limited.

It is obvious that the establishment of museums started late in

Yorubaland (Ojo 1969: 12). The process of collecting religious materials from local people and shrines also required a lot of financial and political support (Awolalu 1996: 114). The quality of materials collected and the conditions that they were kept in was not ideal (Awe and Albert 1995: 1-2). The authenticity of the materials collected could not be ascertained, because the original ones remained untouchable because of the spiritual implications on the community as a whole. Original religious materials are sometimes charmed with local power and the priests kept them away from government collecting agents (MacGaffey 2000: 229).

Yoruba Christians and Moslems who wanted to distance themselves from their family's idol-worship and multi-generation collections would purposely destroy their religious materials (Peel 1967: 292-306). The intention of these converts was to erase the memory of their past religious affiliation from their family and community (Beier 1972). Because such items were in personal collections, people had the right to do whatever they wanted with them. Other religious materials that were not destroyed by these converts had been looted by professional thieves and sold overseas (Beier 1972: 32).

Most of the religious materials left in the Yoruba museums are not properly preserved from contamination and destruction by natural elements. Weather conditions have had an impact on a few religious materials. Yorubaland is too humid for the materials to survive past four generations. Insects, such as termites, feed on the surviving materials. Occasionally, other materials that are left unattended are affected by rain and floods. In the dry season, fire consumes the leftover ones (Ojo 1969: 12). Wood carved images are the most affected items (Ojo 1979: 334).

So far, we have noted that informants, local priests and materials from museums can be used in understanding the history of the Yoruba religion. But one should not rely solely on one at the expense of other in accessing the history of an oral religion.

9
Mythological Studies in the History of Religion

Last in our discussion of Osun Osogbo is the summary of anthropologists and sociologists in understanding the history of the Yoruba religion and its world view.

A. Ferdinand de Saussure (1857-1913)

Ferdinand de Saussre is a Swiss linguist whose insights into the structural linguistics led to more interest in structuralism around the world. His intention is to discard the humanistic assumptions on the use of language. He argues that literature is made of language. To understand how literature works, one must have some ideas about how language itself works.

Saussure has had a great influence on the development of structuralism and semiology through his study of the developments of signs within society as a structural system of relationships among words. His interest in the universal structure of language, as applied to all languages, is a signifying system. His influence in the debates of structuralism and semiology gives him the idea that there is a set of units and rules that create a method of conveying meaning to writer, reader and listeners. In all languages there are codes that are understandable only to those who have made conscious efforts to learn them; for example, sign language, traffic signs and many more. One can say the same thing in relation to the origin, structure and meaning of myth.

Saussure speaks of the social nature of speech and writing. Whether complex or simple, there are links between language and power. Ignorance of the existence of language is not an excuse for violating the underlying principles of a system. Saussure distinguishes *langue*, the French word for language, as a unit, system and rule of language as a whole. The second unit of language structure is *parole*, which is the French word for speech. People are familiar with the *parole* because it appeals to our senses more than the *langue*. The structuralists' effort is to analyze how a word is associated with an idea or thing within a given community. The communities vary according to geographical, cultural, religious or professional groups.

The creation of myth is based on the use of the structure of language. Language originates from human thought. Myth, therefore, is a product of various phenomena and sometimes the basic characteristics of the human mind that is expressed in language. Every individual and culture has a tendency to create myth. A greater number of myths often lead to an increase in writing and documentation of them.

Langue may be studied for its formal properties, but it cannot be understood apart from its particular uses. *Langue* expresses the contents of myth. It would take a scientific linguist to establish the significance of myth. To make myth relevant, the linguist would have to focus on the *langue*, for *langue* is the system or structure of a language, that is, its words, syntax, parts of speech, poetical devices, meanings and grammar. Myth helps us to comprehend magic, imagination, dreams, intuition and the unconscious. It helps us to establish a meaningful context for human existence and action. Language and literature are rich in myth. As Ferdinand de Saussure laid the ground work of structuralism, Claude Levi-Strauss and other lingusist anthropologists started building on it.

B. Claude Levi-Strauss (1908-2009)

Levi-Strauss is a famous French anthropologist who applies the structuralist approach to his study of myth. He finds the same structural relationship between ritual and myth. Myth is a delusion of history as he perceives it from the psychological point of view. Levi-Strauss emphasizes the rational orientation of pre-industrial peoples to conclude that myth is a product of the primitive's intellectual exercise. It is a result of their efforts to make sense out of disorderly universe. It is a signifying system in any culture that contains signs which can be read and interpreted for a significant reason. It is a way the signifiers are connected to the signs of myth. Myth is anonymous. It is practically impossible to know the origin of any one of them (Levi-Strauss 1975: 18). Levi-Strauss does not concern himself with the cultural context of myth. Every myth can be explained independent of its cultural and social context. Myth may not have historical validity but it has a consistent pattern which is called structure.

Levi-Strauss argues that myth has certain mythic motifs and structures which are transcultural. The structure of myth is a system of composition that shows a consistent organizing principle in all of them. Levi-Strauss applies the structuralist approach to myth as material for academic research. In order to properly explain a myth, the contents of other myths must be considered. He finds inter-relations among myths. There are sub-themes in them. It is therefore the task of a structuralist first to find these smallest components of resemblance in myths, which could be in a form of language, subject, location, action or an event, and then focus on that particular theme and build a thesis on it. For Levi-Strauss, myth constitutes a particular code, a sign system that requires explanations. Its reality lies under the surface whether we are consciously aware of it or not.

Myth is repetitive and that is why it is not boring to the hearer or the narrator. It has the tendency to give a similar message over and over again without losing its structure. It may appear in different versions, with the possibility of omitting or adding particular information. Scholars can only explain the message of a myth by treating various versions and decoding its messages for the community. Usually, there are dozens of versions of a major myth in Yoruba religions. One thing about all these versions is that each of them would claim itself to be the original one. Often, the earlier ones are thought to be better or more reliable versions when it comes to academic analysis. It is right to also mention that there is no significance attached to its chronological or historical time frame. Structurally, time is reversible. It does not make any difference with which version one begins in research.

Levi-Staruss favors the structuralist interpretation of myth because one has to determine the value of its signs. Myth is a source of power if one could differentiate how one sign is different from all other signs in the system. Myth is used to justify individual interests in situations of conflict and uncertainty. Myth is a pseudo-science of the primitive mind; therefore, myth can not be considered as a science proper. The main purpose of myth is to satisfy the intellectual quest of people; the function of myth is not to solve practical problems. Myth provides material for human-beings to reflect upon, to analyse and to classify events in life. Exercising of mind is a universal need that is in pre-scientific and scientific people.

As we have read from the previous chapters, in the Yoruba community myth is translatable into any language and culture. Myth remains meaningful even after undergoing many translations and transliterations. The significance of myth is in its message, not in context, language, time or sequence. Myth offers us a chance to discover timeless universal human truths by using a methodology that is objective. It discloses what all humans share by virtue of being human. But the truth to be discovered is under the level of structure for those who are determined to find out.

Myth helps us to reconcile the contradictions or oppositions in a cultural or social context. To understand the logic of myth one has to do a scientific analysis of each unit of myth, after which, one's interpretation would have the same kind of authenticity that scientific analysis has. Such analysis may also stimulate further mechanical researches on the subject. It is what sustains kinship system. It governs the economic, educational, religious and social relations in primitive societies. It gives people within the kinship the authority similar to the scientific authority.

Levi-Strauss argues for the function of myth not only in religion but also in music (in Okpewho: ix). Music also sustains the memory of myth. Myth can be used to impress in people the moral truth that wickedness and cruelty will be punished, and righteousness will be rewarded (Okpewho: 5). Myth is traditional knowledge that is conveyed in the seriousness of its story. Myth is the idea of the personification of fictive concepts. As it becomes clear, Levi-Strauss's theories have had a great influence on Rudolf Bultmann's theory of myth.

C. Carl G. Jung (1875-1961)

Carl Jung has a similar view of myth as Freud. His definition of myth is influenced by his previous works on dreams and the subconscious. He identifies dream patterns in myth. Dreaming is common among people of different generations and geographical locations. He speaks of the mythology of the psyche. Psyche is the shadow animal and animus, which is another word for soul. Jung emphasizes the collective unconscious of the primitive people. Jung views the contents of the unconscious positively, even religiously. His theory is psychological because he deals with psyche. His intention is to elevate the study of mythology to a scientific level in discussion and analysis; therefore, he provides the psychological analysis of myth.

The origin of myth starts with natural instinct. Indispensable intermediate states of mind generate mythological idea and narrative.

Mythology comes out of the common human images of collective unconscious. This collective unconscious is a psychological basis from which all human life derives meaning. Myth resides in the human psyche, the world of the archetypes.

Jung defines myth as story about heroes interacting with the gods. Myth is the origins and history of consciousness. Myth is the narrative of archetypal images. The actual meaning of myth is contained in the depths of the self which are depicted in narrative. Myth represents the unconscious archetypal, instinctual, structures of the mind. Human instincts are the same universally; therefore, the collective unconscious is the same for all human beings of all cultures.

Jung states that myth-forming structural elements are present in the unconscious psyche (Jung 2001: 85). Myth is the colourful and poetical use of language in a narrative. Myth and symbols have much in common. The structure of myth starts in the human mind as one engages in mythmaking. Myth occupies a tiny island of consciousness in the midst of the vast space of human unconsciouness. Human thought and belief originate from the unconscious aspect of human being. Jung emphasizes the significance of image over the word. The language of the unconsciousness does not do justice to unconsciouness.

Archetypes represent different aspects of the human instinctual structure. The concept of archetypes has an historical link to the term '*an imago*', for it also finds its expression in symbols. The archetypes are inferred from the manifestation of typical symbols found in myth and other forms of literature. Archetypes appear in myths and fairytales (Jung 2001: 86). An archetypal image can be perceived in dreams, visions and fantasies. The image of the archetypal can also be represented in terms of the cultural codes. It is a depiction of symbols. A single archetype is specific to each situation, but a single archetype can have an indefinite number of expressions. Archetypes, the motifs of myth, also find representation in visual presentation, such as drama, music and verbal expression. There can be more than one motif in a myth, but if there is, all motifs usually link in a sequence to form the myth.

Jung identifies archetypes of the collective unconsciousness. The unconscious contains the forgotten experiences of the individual from birth forward. In other words, to tap into the unconciousness, one has to think back through one's entire self-history. Archetypes express themselves through images as a mirror reflects images. The images are suggestive representations of the exact images.

Jung almost equates archetypes and instincts. Human beings are creatures of instinct. Instinct forms the major part of humans' mental ability. Within a community, the unconsciouness content of an individual, or a collection of people, is passed on to the next generation through a sharing of information, interaction or even by birth. The forgotten past is preserved in the form of archetypes.

Jung's discussions on the function of myth take into consideration the role of myth for individual and society as a whole. Myth serves as a rule of tribal history handed down from one generation to another (Jung 2001: 86). Myth is used to convey some emotional message and sharing of experience with one's associates. Every myth contains the power of revealing some unforeseen or neglected aspect of the human psyche.

D. Mircea Eliade (1907-1986)

Mircea Eliade's work on the history of religions, which was first published in English in 1954, established his reputation around the world. He makes a compelling argument for the varieties of religious expressions and activities in world religions. His book, *the Myth of the Eternal Return or, Cosmos and History*, "examines the fundamental concepts of archaic societies - the societies which, although they are conscious of a certain form of "history," make every effort to disregard it" (Eliade 1971: ix). He thinks the archaic societies revolt against concrete historical accounts.

Eliade's view of the nature of myth in religious studies is basically antihistorical. In interpreting myth, the structures, meanings and significance of each myth must all be examined. To interpret myth and religion, one must do justice to the complex structure of both subjects. Myth is a collective participation of a community in recognizing common symbols. It is a special collective thinking process of a community. It usually tells us the actions of the supernaturals. The purpose of one's desire to know the details of a myth is to be able to control it.

The collective memory of each community is ahistorical because there is a tendency to transform specific historical individuals and events into a myth. The people of modern societies do not value myth as such. But in archaic societies, specific historical figures and events easily acquired mythic status. Eliade says "for the man of the archaic societies, the Cosmos too has a "history"" (Eliade 1971: xiv). The history is sacred and it can only be transmitted through myths.

Myth expresses the total belief system of a society. It provides a stereotypic form and information of the people. Because the meaning and function of myth may vary from one person to another, it requires considerable effort to discover myth's significance for the community as a whole. Part of the problem of working with myth is that the linear concept of time cannot or does not exist in myth. For Eliade, myth's nature, meaning and significance are minimal in religious studies.

Myth repeats the belief system of societies. It preserves and transmits "the paradigms, the exemplary models" of the archaic societies from one generation to another (Eliade 1971: xiv). According to Eliade, myth is a way of dealing with the problems and solutions of archaic societies, particularly the Oriental people, (Eliade 1971: x).

E. Rudolf Bultmann (1884-1976)

Rudolf Bultmann is a biblical scholar who first got me thinking about the mythological figures in the Yoruba religion. Personally, Bultmann's works on the mythological Jesus motivated me to consider applying myth in a treatment of the significance of Yoruba gods in religious studies. Bultmann has a romantic view of myth. He defines myth in the way the science of history and of religion, by saying that myth is "the report of an occurrence or an event in which supernatural, superhuman forces or persons are at work (which explains why it is often defined simply as history of gods) (Bultmann 1984: 95). He sees different underlying structures of the universe, when he writes "The world picture of the New Testament is a mythical world picture. The world is a three-story structure, with earth in the middle, heaven above it, and hell below it" (Bultmann 1984: 1). He defines the role of myth as "not to give an objective world picture; what is expressed in it, rather, is how we human beings understand ourselves in our world" (Bultmann 1984: 9). Myth talks about transcendent powers of demons, gods and inanimate objects. It talks about transcendent reality and power operating in a spatially distant time. Myth, therefore, should be interpreted in anthropological terms and not in cosmological terms because it makes gods into human beings, and makes human beings gods. For us to understand this phenomena one must make effort to demythologize myth. If one looks at myth, what it displays is the faith that is familiar to us. This is his mythical world picture and where salvation of the New Testament must be proclaimed. Bultmann adopts an existential view from Levi-Strauss' and Marin Heidegger's analysis of human existence (Bultmann 1984: 22-23).

Conclusion

In summary, myth is a pre-scientific understanding of the universe. The purpose of myth is not to present an objective picture of reality. Eliade says "for archaic man, reality is a function of the initiation of a celestial archetype" (Eliade: 5). A sense of reality is affirmed in one's life through participation in initiations. It is a way that man understands himself as a part of the universe. It is an expression of who he is in relation to other things around him. Therefore, "reality manifests itself as force, effectiveness, and duration" of initiations (Eliade: 11). Myth is created around intitations as expressions of man's awareness that he is not lord of his own being. As human acts acquire effectiveness, they are repeated again and again as exemplary models for the community to follow. For every act has a definite meaning to a structuralist (Eliade: 28).

What do these structuralists theories share in common and how is each different from another? Although the similarities and differences are not the focus of this book, but the following summary of the various structuralist theories is useful for us to know. Bultmann demythologizes only to remythologize. The theories of Levi-Strauss and Carl Jung are ahistorical. Jung sees myth as simply a collection of public dreams and an artistic reflection of what goes on in an individual's mind. Jung's approach to myth is reductionistic and deterministic. Whatever theories one adopts, the study of myth is a serious and important pursuit. Myths have much to tell us about community belief and practice of people as it is revealed in our study of Osun's myths.

Structuralism is a human science which seeks to explain, in a systematic and logical way, the structure behind human experience and behavior. The common uses of the word structure do not necessarily imply structural activities like erecting a building. Stucturalists attempt to discover the underlying principles in myth. The goal is to find the structural system of classification myths into different groups either topical or geographical.

For a structuralist, the world as we experience it consists of two fundamental levels, the visible and the invisible structures. What we see, hear, touch, smell and taste on the visible level is superficial. The invisible world consists of that underlying fundamental meaning whether we are aware of it or not. By understanding the underlying principle, one would be able to appreciate the visible phenomena.

Structuralists believe that structures are products of mind, and therefore it will take human mind to understand the two levels of structure in order to make sense of the chaotic world. Human thought has a structuring mechanism that generates ideas about things and people. The structures we are trying to understand are actually innate structures of human consciousness. There are so many of these structures that we need to develop a mature conceptual system in order to organize and understand their underlying meanings and significance in each community.

A descriptive structuralist approach has been helpful to us. Our objective perspective of Osun as well as our experience and perception become reliable methods of knowing her importance in Yoruba worship. The empirical approach is the way human beings project themselves into what they experience, thereby creating knowledge out of their own preconceptions. This is a method by which a researcher interprets the world view of the people he or she is studying without imposing one personal social reality on the people one is understudying. It is expected to be done from the objective perspective. The question raised against experiential claims of empirical research is, can their works stand under rational scrutiny? It is essential that every assumption be avoided, and one should never impose one concept of social reality on the topic.

Theory of myth encourages us to think about the structure and function of myth. The method we have used here is the descriptive method, involving a process, principles and procedures by which we approach the subject, Osun. This examination of myth reveals the ways people described themselves and their practices of religious beliefs.

In conclusion, it can be stated that the study of the myths of Osun is one of the reliable approaches for understanding the Yoruba religion in the Old and the New Worlds. Myths offer significant historical and religious information for believers and scholars in understanding people around the world. This book does not, in any way, cover all areas of Osun. The influence of Osun in Europe, Asia and Arab countries are out there for further studies. The influences of Osun on teenagers would also be a good area of study for people who are interested in Yoruba religious studies. Interestingly, Catherine Wishart has briefly mentioned Osun as one of the goddesses that guides girls in the area of magic, makeup and meditation (Wishart 2003: 267-275). Osun in Hollywood could be yet another area of study. Psychologists could psychologize the actions and reactions during the Osun festival. Linguists could compare and contrast the differences in the use of Yoruba language in Osogbo and the New World. Architects could study the images at the Osun shrines. Studies on Osun could be inter-departmental studies. In a nutshell, Osun is an African-initiated religious worship that is sustained in other parts of the world.

Bibliography

Abimbola, Kola
   2006 *Yoruba Culture: A Philosophical Account*. Great Britain: Iroko Academic Publishers.
Abimbola, Wande
   1977 *Ifa Divination Poetry*. New York: NOK Publishers.
Adegbola, Ade E. A. (ed.).
   1983 *Traditional Religion in West Africa*. Accra: Asempa Publishers.
Abiodun, Rowland
   2001 "Power: Osun, the Seventeenth Odu." in Murphy, Joseph M and Mei-Mei Sanford, eds. *Osun Across the Waters: A Yoruba Goddess in Africa and the Americas*. Bloomington: Indiana University.
Adeoye, C. L.
   1979 *Asa ati Ise Yoruba*. Nigeria: Oxford University Press.
Adeyemo, Tokunbo
   1979 *Salvation in African Tradition*. Nairobi: Evangel Publishing House.
Afolayan, Michael O.
   2005 "Aabo Oro: The Indigenous Language of Education in Yoruba" in Toyin Falola and Ann Genova (eds.) *Yoruba Creativity: Fiction, Language, Life, and Songs*. Trenton, NJ: African World Press.
Ajayi, Jacob F. Ade
   1965 *Christian Missions in Nigeria 1841-91: The Making of a New Elite* London: Longmans.
Ajayi, Jacob F. Ade and Robert Smith
   1964 *Yoruba Warfare in the Nineteenth Century*. Ibadan, Nigeria: Cambridge University Press, in Association with the Institute of African Studies, University of Ibadan.
Ajayi Omofolabo S.
   1998 *Yoruba Dance African*. World Press, INC.
Akinjogbin, Adeagbo
   1998 *and Peace in Yorubaland 1793-1893*. Nigeria: Heinemann Education Books.
Akintoye, S. A.
   1971 *Revolution and Power Politics Yorubaland: Ibadan Expansion and the Rise of Ekitiparapo*. Ile-Ife: Department of Histories, University of Ife, Humanities Press.
Allen, Gouglas
   2002 *Myth and Religion in Mircea Eliade*. London: Routledge.
   2005 "Phenomenology of Religion" in John R. Hinnells (ed.), *The Routledge Companion to the Study of Religion*. London: Routledge.
Awe, B. and Albert, O.
   1995 "Historical Development of Osogbo" in: *Model of Growing African Town*" C. O. Adepegba (Ed). Institute of African Studies University of Ibadan, Nigeria.
Awolalu, J. Omosade *Yoruba Beliefs and Sacrificial Rites*. London: Longman,
   1979/1996 Athelia Henrietta Press, INC, New York.
Awolalu, Omosade J. and Dopomu Adelumo.
   1979 *West African Traditional Religion*. Ibadan: Onibooje Publishing.
Awolalu Omosade J.
   1996 *Yoruba Beliefs and Sacrificial Rites*. Athelia Henrietta Press, INC, New York.
Ayandele, E. A.
   1966 *The Missionary Impact on Modern Nigeria 1842-1914: A Political and Social Analysis*. London: Longman, Green.
Badejo, Diedre L.

1996 *Osun Seegesi: the Elegant Deity of Wealth, Power, and Femininity.* Trenton, New Jersey: African World Press.

Bakewell, Peter
1997 *A History of Latin America.* Carlton, Victoria: Blackwell Publishing Limited.

Barrett, B. D.
1968 *Schism and Renewal in Africa; An Analysis of Six Thousand Contemporaries Religious Movement.* London: Oxford University Press.

Bascom, Jean and Mellive J. Herskovits, eds.
1959 *Continuity and Change in Africa Cultures.* Chicago: University of Chicago Press.

Bascom, William Russell
1966 *The Origin of Life and Death: African Creation Myths.* London, Ibadan (e.t.c): Heinemann.
1970 *Yoruba Poetry: an Authority of Traditional Poems.* Cambridge (Eng.): University Press.
1971 *The Origin of the Yoruba.* Lagos: University of Lagos.
1972 *Shango in the New World African and Afro-American Research Institute.* ###
1973 *African Art in Cultural Perspective.* New York: Norton and Company.
1981 *Contributions of Folkloristics.* Meerut, India: Folklore Institute, Archana Publications.
1993 *Sixteen Cowries: Yoruba Divination from Africa to the New World.* First Midland Book.

Bascom, William Russell and Gerald Moore eds.
1963 *The Modern Poetry from Africa.* Hamondsworth: Penguin Books.

Bastide, Roger
1960 *The African Religions of Brazil: Toward a Society of the Interpenetration of Civilizations.* The Johns Hopkins University Press, Baltimore and London.

Beier, Ulli
1971 *The Return of the God, Sacred Art of Sussane.* Ibadan, Nigeria: University of Ibadan, Institute of African Studies.
1980 *Yoruba Myths.* Compiled and introduced by Ulli Beier; illustrated by Georgina Beier. Cambridge, New York: Cambridge University Press.

Benitez-Rojo, Antonio
1996 *The Repeating Island: The Caribbean and the Postmodern Perspective,* translated by James Maraniss. Durham and London: Duke University Press.

Bjorling, Joel
1988 *Consulting Spirits: A Bibliography.* Westport, CT: Greenwood Press.

Bonnefoy, Yves
1991 *American, African, and Old European Mythologies.* Chicago: The University of Chicago.

Boris, Wisemann
2000 *Introducing Levi-Strauss and Structural Anthropology.* NY: Totem Books.

Bourdillon, Michael
1995 "Anthropological Approaches to the Study of African Religion" in *The Study of Religions in Africa: Past, Present and Prospects,* eds. Jan Platvoet, James Cox and Jacob Olupona, Cambridge: Roots and Branches.

Brandon, George
1997 *Santeria from Africa to the New World: the Dead Sell Memories.* Bloomington: Indiana University Press.

Bultmann, Rudolf
1960 *Jesus Christ and Mythology.* London: SCM.
1984 *New Testament and Mythology and Other Basic Writings.*

Philadelphia: Fortress Press.
Cameron, Sarah
   2004 *Cuba*. Bath, UK: Footprint.
Carbrera, Lydia
   2004Afro-Cuban Tales. Translated by Alberto Hernandez-Chiroldes and Lauren
       Yoder. Lincoln: University of Nebraska.
Castellanons, Isabel
   2001 "A River of Many Turns: The Polysemy of Ochun in Afro-Cuban Tradition" in
       Murphy, Joseph M and Mei-Mei Sanford, eds. *Osun Across the Waters: A*
       Yoruba Goddess in Africa and the Americas. Bloomington: Indiana University.
       Centre for African Settlement Studies and Development. *Urban Poverty and*
   1993Environment in Nigeria Inner Cities: Lessons from a Case Study, Osogbo. Ibadan: The Centre
       Press.
Christensen, Thomas G.
   1990 *An African Tree of Life*. New York: Orbis Books.
Cicora, Mary A.
   1998 *Mythology as Metaphor: Romantic Irony, Critical Theory, and Wagner's Ring*. Oxford:
       Greenwood Press, 1998.
Considine, John Joseph
   1958 *New Horizons in Latin America*. New York, Maryknoll: Maryknoll
       Publications.
Courlander, Harold
   1975 *A Treasury of African Folklore: The Oral Literature, Traditions, Myths*. New York, NY:
       Crown Publishers.
Cox, J. L.
   1992 Expressing the Sacred: an Introduction to the Phenomenology of Religion.
       Harare: University of Zimbabwe Publications.
   1996 "Methodological Considerations Relevant to Understanding African Indigenous
       Religions," in *The Study of Religions in Africa: Past, Present and Prospects*, eds. Jan Platvoet, James Cox
and Jacob Olupona, Cambridge: Roots and Branches.
Csapo, Eric
   2005 *Theories of Mythology*. Oxford: Blackwell Publishing.
Curtin, Philip D.
   1964, 1967 *African Remembered: Narratives by West Africans from the Era of Slave*
       Trade. Madison: University of Wisconsin Press.
   1969 The Atlantic Slave Trade A Census. The University of Wisconsin Press,
       Madison, Milwaukee, and London.
   1990 The Rise and Fall of the Plantation Complex Essays in Atlantic History
       Cambridge University Press, Cambridge, New York, Port Chester, Melbourne, Sydney.
Davies, Alan
   1988 *Infected Christianity: A Study of Modern Racism*. Kingston, Ontario: McGill-
       Queen's University Press.
De Graft, J. C.
   2002 "Roots in African Drama and Theatre" in *Black Theatre: Ritual Performance in*
       the African Diaspora. Edited by Paul Carter Harrison, Victor Leo Walker II,
       and Gus Edwards. Philadelphia: Temple University Press.
De La Torre, Miguel
   2004 *Santeria: The Beliefs and Rituals of a Growing Religion in America*. Grand

Rapids, Michigan: Eerdmans Publishing.

Denzer, LaRay
    1988   *The Iyalode in Ibadan Politics and Society, c. 1850–1997*. In honour of Professor Bolanle Awe, Ibadan: Publication of Humanities Research Centre Ibadan.

Durosimi, Eldred Jones
    1997   *African Literature Today: Journal of Criticism*. Number 1, 2, 3, 4, with index. Heinemann: Africana Publishing Corporation.

Eugenio Matibag
    1996   *Afro-Cuban Religious Experience*. Miami: University Press of Florida.

Eliade, Mircea
    1954, 1971   *The Myth of the Eternal Return or, Cosmos and History*. Translated by William R. Trask. New York: Princeton University Press.
    1964   *Myth and Reality*. London: Allen and Union.
    1968   *Myths, Dreams and Mysteries*. London: Fountain.

Evans, David
    1999   "The Reinterpretation of African Musical Instruments in the United States" In Isidore Okpewho, Carole Boyce Davies, and Ali A. Mazuri, The African Diaspora *African Origins and New world Identities*. Bloomington: Indiana University.

Fadipe, N. A.
    1970   *The Sociology of the Yoruba*. Ibadan: Ibadan University Press.

Fagan, Eduard
    1996   "Roman-Dutch Law in its South African Historical Context" in Reinhard Zimmermann and Daniel Visser (eds.) *Southern Cross: Civil Law and Common Law in South Africa*. New York: Clarendon Press.

Falola, Toyin and Ann Genova eds.
    2005   *Orisha: Yoruba Gods and Spiritual Identity in Africa and the Diaspora*. Trenton New Jersey: Africa World Press.

Farrow, Stephens S.
    1996   *Fancies, and Fetich, or Yoruba Paganism*. Brooklyn, New York: Athelia Henrietta Press.

Fatunmbi, A. F.
    1993   *Oshun: Ifa and the Spirit of the River*. Bronx, NY: Original Publications.

Fischer, Sibylle
    2004   *Modernity Disavowed: Haiti and the Cultures of Slavery in the Age of Revolution*. Durham, NC: Duke University Press.

Frobenius, Leo
    1913   *The Voice of Africa*: Vols. 1-2, London: Hutchinson.

Garcia Cortex, Julio
    1-2005   *The Osha: Secrets of the Yoruba-Lucumi-Santeria Religion in the United States and the Americas; Initiation, Rituals, Ceremonies, Orishas, Divination, Plants, Sacrifices, Cleansings, Songs*. Brooklyn New York: Athleia Henrietta.

Gilkey, Langdon
    1970   *Religion and the Scientific Future*. New York: Harper and Row Publishers.

Gira, Pomba
    2004   "Spirits of Brazil" in *Queering Creed Spiritual Traditions: Lesbian, Gay, Bisexual, and Transgender*. Edited by John P. De Cecco. Binghampton, NY: Park Press.

Gleason, Judith
    1973   *Orisa: the Gods of Yorubaland*. New York: Atheneum.

Gonzalez-Wippler, Migene
   1989 *Santeria: The Religion, Faith, Rites, Magic*. St. Paul, MN: Llewellyn Publication.
Gomez, Michael Angelo
   2005 *Reversing Sail: A History of the African Diaspora*. Cambridge, UK: Cambridge University Press.
Hawkins, Odie
   1994 *Lost Angeles: The Conflict Between Korean-American and African-American Cultures in Los Angeles*. Los Angeles: Holloway House Publishing Company.
Hayward, Victor E. W. (ed.)
   1963 *African Independent Church Movements*. London: Edinburgh House Press.
Herskovits, Melville J.
   1947 Trinidad Village. New York: A. A. Knopf.
   1966 *The New World Negro*. Edited by: Herskovits, Frances S. Indiana University Press, Bloomington.
Herskovits, Melville J. and Frances S. Herskovits
   1948 *Man and His Works: The Science of Cultural* Anthropology. New York: Knopf.
Henry, Frances
   2003 *Reclaiming African Religions in Trinidad: The Socio-Political Legitimation of the Orisha and Spiritual Baptist Faiths*. Kingston, Jamaica: The University of the West Indies Press.
Henry, Paget
   2000 *Caliban's Reason: Introducing Afro-American Philosophy: Caribbean Perspective*. New York, NY: Routledge.
Hexham, Irving
   1981 *The Irony of Apartheid: the Struggle for National Independence of Afrikaner*. Lewiston, NY: Edwin Mellen Press.
   1993 *The Concise Dictionary*. Vancouver, Regent: Regent College Publishing.
Hexham, Irving and Karla Poewe
   1986 *Understanding Cults and New Age Religion*. Grand Rapids, MI: William B. Eerdmans.
Houk, James T.
   1995 *Spirits, Blood, and Drums The Orisha Religion in Trinidad*. Temple University Press, Philadelphia.
Hugh, Thomas
   1997 *The Slave Trade: The Story of the Atlantic Slave Trade 1440-1870*. New York, NY: Simon and Schuster.
Idowu, E. Bolaji
   1973 *African Traditional Religions*. New York: Orbis Books.
Inikori, Joseph E.
   1997 "Slaves or Serfs? A Comparative Study of Slavery and Serfdom in Europe and Africa" *African Diaspora: African Origins and New World Identities*. Bloomington: Indiana University Press.
Isidore Okewho
   1999 Carole Boyce Davies, and Ali A. Mazuri, *The African Diaspora African Origins and New World Identities*. Indianapolis: Indiana University Press.
Jiboye, Adesoji
   1999 *An Appraisal of Housing Standard. A Case Study of Moremi Estate, Ile - Ife*. Unpublished Independent Research. Department of U. R. P., Obafemi Awolowo University, Ile-Ile.
Johnston, Harry Sir.

1969 The *Negro in the New World,* Johnson Reprint Corporation, New York and London.
Johnson, Samuel
   1970 *The History of the Yorubas: From the Earliest Times to the Beginning of the British Protectorate*. O. Johnson, editor. Westport, Conn.: Negro University Press.
Johnson, Paul Christopher
   2002 *The Transformation of Brazilian Candomble: Secrets, Gossip, and Gods*. New York: Oxford University Press.
Johnson, Samuel
   1921 *The History of the Yorubas*. Lagos: CMS Bookshops.
Johnson, Samuel and O. Johnson
   1970 *The History of the Yorubas: From the Earliest Times to the Beginning of the British Protectorate*. Westport, Connecticut: Negro University Press.
Joseph M. Murphy and Mei-Mei Sanford
   2001 *Osun Across the Water A Yoruba Goddess in Africa and the Americas.* Indiana University Press.
Jung, Carl Gustan
   1953 *The Collected Works of C. G. Jung*. Volume 8, edited by Sir Herbert Read. Michael Fordham, and Gerhard Alder. London: Routledge and Kegan Paul
   1959 *The Collected Works of C. G. Jung*. Volume 9, edited by Sir Herbert Read. Michael Fordham, Gerhard Alder, and William McGuire. London: Routledge and Kegan Paul
   1960 *The Collected Works of C. G. Jung*. Volume 8, edited by Sir Herbert Read. Michael Fordham, and Gerhard Alder. London: Routledge and Kegan Paul.
Jung, Carl Gustan and Karl Kerenyi
   2001 *Science of Mythology: Essays on the Divine Child and the Mysteries of Eleusis.* Second edition. Routledge.
Kaldera, Raven
   2004 *Myth Astrology: Exploring Planets and Pantheon*. St. Paul, MN: Llewellyn Publications.
Knight, Franklin W.
   2003, 2001 "Slavery and Transformation of Society in Cuba." In B. W. Higman, Carl Campbell and Patrick Bryan (eds.), *Slavery, Freedom and Gender: The Dynamics of Caribbean Society*. Kingston, Jamaica: University of the West Indies.
Kopytoff, Igor and Suzanne Miers
   1977 "African 'Slavery' as an Institution of Marginality," in Suzanne Miers and Igor Kopytoff, eds. *Slavery in Africa: Historical and Anthropological Perspectives*, Madison: University of Wisconsin Press.
Krapf-Askari, Eva
   1969 *Yoruba Towns and Cities*. Oxford: Clarendon Press.
Ladle, Jane
   1999 *Insight Guides: Brazil*. New York: Langescheidt Publishers.
Law, Robin C.
   1977 *The Oyo Empire 1600-1836*. Oxford: Clarendon Press.
Lawson, Thomas E.
   1985 *Religions of Africa*. San Francisco: Harper and Row.
Lele, Ocha'ni
   2000 *The Secrets of Afro-Cuban Divination: How to Cast the Dilogun, the Oracle of the Orishas*. Rochester, Vt.: Destiny Books.
   2001 *Obi: Oracle of Cuban Santeria.* Rochester, Vt.: Destiny Book.

2003 *The Dilogun: The Orishas, Proverbs, Sacrifices, and Prohibitions of Cuban Santeria.* Rochester, Vermont: Destiny Books.

Levi-Strauss, Claude
1962 *Totemism.* Translated by Rodney Needham. Boston: Beacon Press.
1967 "The Story of Asdiwal" translated Nicholas Mann in *The Structural Study of Myth and Totemism.* Edited by Edumnd Leach. Tavistock Publications.
1978 *Myth and Meaning.* Toronto: University of Toronto.

Lima, Robert
1995 *Dark Prisms: Occultism in Hispanic Drama.* Lexington, Kentucky: The University of Kentucky.

Littlewood, Ronald
1993 Pathology and Identity The Work of Mother Earth in Trinidad. Cambridge University Press.

Loewenthal, Kate Miriam and Marco Cinnirella
2003 "Religious Issues in Ethnic Minority Mental Health: Special Reference to Schizophrenia in Afro-Caribbean in Britain: A Systematic Review" in *Main Issues in Mental Health and Race.* Deavi Ndegwa and Dele Olajide eds. Burlington, VT: Ashgate Publishing Company.

Lucas, J. Olumide
1948 *Religion of the Yorubas.* Lagos: C. M. S. Bookshop.

Lum, Kenneth A.
2000 *Praising His Name in the Dance: Spiritual Baptist Faith and Orisha Work in Trinidad, West Indies.* Amsterdam, The Netherlands: Harwood Academic Publishers.

Mabogunje, A. L.
1971 *Owu in Yoruba History.* Ibadan: Ibadan University Press.

MacGaffey, Wyatt
2000 "Art and Spirituality," *African Spirituality: Forms, Meanings, and Expressions (World Spirituality v. 3)* edited by Jacob K. Olupona. New York, New York: The Crossroad Publishing Company.

Marie-Jeanne
2002 *The Goddess in Every Girl: Develop Your Teen Feminine Power.* Rochester, Vermont: Bindu Book.

Mason, Michael Atwood
2002 *Living Santeria – Rituals and Experiences in an Afro-Cuban Religion.* Smithsonian Institution Press, Washington and London.

Matibag, Eugenio
1996 *Afro-Cuban Religious Experience: Cultural Reflections in Narrative.* Gainesville, Florida: University of Florida.

Matory, J. Lorand
2005 *Black Atlantic Religion: Tradition, Transnationalism and Matriarchy in the Afro-Brazilian Candomble.* New Jersey: Princeton University Press.

Mberi, Antar S. K.
1980 *A Song of Harlem.* Clifton, NJ: The Humana Press.

Metraux, Alfred
1960 *Black Peasants and Voodoo,* translated by Peter Lengyel. New York: Universe Books.
1972 *Voodoo in Haiti.* Trans. Hugo Charteris. New York: Schoken Books.

Mbiti, John

1975 *The Prayers of African Religion*. New York: Orbis Books.

Mbon, Friday
   1996 "Some Methodological Issues in the Academic Study of West African Traditional Religions" in *The Study of Religions in Africa: Past, Present and Prospects*, eds. Jan Platvoet, James Cox and Jacob Olupona, Cambridge: Roots and Branches.

Mendelssohn, Jack
   1962 *God, Allah and Juju: Religions in Africa Today*. Boston: Beacon Press.

Middleton, John
   1976 *Myth and Cosmos: Readings in Mythology and Symbolism*. Texas: University of Texas.

Mintz, Sidney W.
   1989 *Caribbean Transformations*. NY: Columbia University Press.

Mitchell, Jolyon P and Sophia Marriage.
   2003 *Mediating Religion: Conversations in Media, Religion and Culture*. NY: T & T Clark Ltd.

Mitchell, Robert C., and Harold W. Turner
   1966 *A Comprehensive Bibliography of Modern African Religious Movements*. Evanston: Northwestern University Press.

Monaghan, Patricia
   2004 *The Goddess Path: Myths, Invocations and Rituals*. St. Paul, Minnesota: Llewellyn Publications.

Morwyn
   2001 *Magic from Brazil: Recipes, Spells, & Rituals*. St. Paul, Minnesota: Llewellyn Publications.

Muller, Max F.
   1873 *Introduction to the Science of Religion*. London: Longmans.

Murphy, Joseph.
   1988 *Santeria: An Africa Religion in North America and Working the Spirit: Ceremonies of the African Diaspora*. Boston: Beacon Press.

Murphy, Joseph M. and Mei-Mei Sanford, eds.
   2001 *Osun Across the Waters: A Yoruba Goddess in Africa on the Americas*. Indiana: Indiana University Press.

Nadel, S. F.
   1954 *Nupe Religion*. London: Routledge and Kegan Limited.

Niven, C. R. A.
   1958 *A Short History of the Yoruba Peoples*. London: Longman.

Oduyoye, Modupe
   1971 *The Vocabulary of Yoruba Religious Discourse*. Ibadan: Daystar Press.

Ojo, Afolabi
   1966 *Yoruba Culture: A Geographical Analysis*. Ile-Ife: University of Ife Press and London: University of London Press.

Ojo, J. R.
   1969 *A Short Illustrated Guide, with an Introduction*. Ile-Ife, Nigeria: University of Ife Press.

Okpewho, Isidore, Carol Boyce Davies, Ali A. Mazuri, eds.
   1999 *African Origins and New World Identities*. Bloomington: Indiana University Press.

Okpewho, Isidore
   1980 "Rethinking Myth."*African Literature Today*. Okpewho, edited Eldred Durosimi Jones: 7-16.

Olugunna, Deji
   1959 *Osogbo, The Origin, Growth and Problems*. Osogbo, Nigeria: Fads' Print Works.

Oluponna, Jacob K (ed.)

1991   *African Traditional Religions in Contemporary Society.* New York: Paragon House.
Oluponna, Jacob
  1973   "Yoruba Sacred Kingship and Civil Religion in Osogbo, Nigeria" in
     Idowu, *African Traditional Religions.* New York: Orbis.
  1996   "The Study of Religions in Nigeria: Past, Present, and Future" in *The Study of
     Religions in Africa: Past, Present and Prospects,* eds. Jan Platvoet, James Cox
     and Jacob Olupona, Cambridge: Roots and Branches.
  1996   "The Study of Religions in West Africa: A Brief Survey" in *The Study of
     Religions in Africa: Past, Present and Prospects,* eds. Jan Platvoet, James Cox
     and Jacob Olupona, Cambridge: Roots and Branches.
  2000   *African Spirituality: Forms, Meanings, and Expressions.* The Crossroad
     Publishing Company, New York.
Omari, Smith Mikkelle
  1994   "Candomble: A Socio-Political Examination of African Religion and Art in
     Brazil" in *Orixa in Candomble Nago.* Thomas D. Berkley, Walter E. A. van
     Beek, and Dennis L. Thomson, eds. Portsmouth, New Hampshire: Heinemann.
Omofolabo, Ajayi S.
  1998   *Yoruba Dance: the Semiotics of Movement and Body Attitude in a Nigerian
     Culture.* Trenton, New Jersey: Africa World Press.
Omoyajowo, J. A.
  1982   *Cherubim and Seraphim: The History of An African Independent Church.* New York: NOK.
Owomoyela, Oyekan
  1997   *Yoruba Trickester Tales.* Lincoln, Nebraska: University of Nebraska.
Owusu, Heike
  2002   *Voodoo Rituals: A User's Guide: A User's Guide.* New York, NY: Sterling
     Publishing Company.
Osogbo Cultural Heritage Council
     Osun Osogbo Festival. Odi-Olowo, Osogbo, Nigeria: Supergraphic Computer Press.
  1998   *Osun Osogbo Festival.* Osun State Nigeria: Kolly Olumide Printers.
Oosthuizen, G. C.
  1989   *The Rastafarians.* Kwazule-Natal: University of Zululand.
Osogbo Cultural Heritage Council
     nd   *Osun Osogbo Festival.* Odi-Olowo, Osogbo: Supergraphic Computer Press.
Oyal'eti, Iyal'ocha Oloya
  2000   *The Three Doors of Ocha: An African-American Guide to the
     Philosophic Principles and Psychological Concepts of Occultism in Practice of
     African Based Traditions in the New World.* Hudson, NY.: Bush Woman Press.
Oyekan Owomoyela
         1999   "Folklore to Literature: The Route From Roots in The African World"
by   Oyekan Owomoyela in Okpewho, Isidore, Carol Boyce Davies, Ali A. Mazuri, eds. *African
     Origins and New World Identities.* Bloomington: Indiana University.
  1994   *History of Osogbo.* Osogbo, Nigeria: Igbalaye Press Limited.
Palmie, Stephan
  2002   *Wizards and Scientists Explorations in Afro-Cuban Modernity and
     Tradition.* Drake University Press, Durham and London.
Park, Mungo
  1813   *Travels in the Interior Districts of Africa,* New York: Evert Duyckinck.
Parrinder, Geoffery

1949 *West African Religion: Illustrated from the Beliefs and Practices of the Yoruba, Ewe, Akan, and Kindred Peoples*. Epworth Press.
1953 *Religion in an African City*. Westport, Connecticut: Negro Universities Press.
1962 *African Traditional Religion*. Greenwood Press Publishers, Westport, Connecticut.
1969 *Africa's Three Religions*. London: Sheldon Press.
1976 *West African Psychology: A Comparative Study of Psychological and Religious Thought*. Lutterworth Press, London.

Patterson, Orlando
    1982 *Slavery and Social Death A Comparative Study*. Harvard University Press, Cambridge, Massachusetts, and London, England.

Pearl, Leon
    1963 *Four Philosophical Problems: God, Freedom, Mind and Perception*. New York: Harper and Row.

Peel, J. D. Y.
    1967/1968 *Aladura: A Religious Movement Among the Yoruba*. London: Oxford University Press.

Plavoet, Jan G., James L. Cox & Jacob Kehinde Olupona (eds.)
    1996 *The Study of Religions in Africa: Past, Present and Prospects*, eds. Jan Platvoet, James Cox and Jacob Olupona, Cambridge: Roots and Branches.

Platvoet, Jan G.
    1996 "From Object to Subject" in *The Study of Religions in Africa: Past, Present and Prospects*, eds. Jan Platvoet, James Cox and Jacob Olupona, Cambridge: Roots and Branches.
    1996 "The Religions of Africa in their Historical Order" in *The Study of Religions in Africa: Past, Present and Prospects*, eds. Jan Platvoet, James Cox and Jacob Olupona, Cambridge: Roots and Branches.

Platvoet, Jan G. and Jacob K. Olupona
    1996 "Perspectives on the Study of Religions in Sub-Saharan African" in *The Study of Religions in Africa: Past, Present and Prospects*, eds. Jan Platvoet, James Cox and Jacob Olupona, Cambridge: Roots and Branches.

Pradel, Lucie
    2000 *African Beliefs in the New World*. Trenton, NJ: African World Press.

Ranger, T. O and Kimambo I. N. eds.
    1972 *The Historical Study of African Religion (with Special Reference to East and Central Africa)*. London: Heinemann.

Ray, Benjamin C.
    2000 *African Religious Symbol, Ritual, and Community*. New Jersey: Prentice Hall.

Ribeiro dos Santos, Ieda Machado
    2001 "Nesta Cidade Todo Mundo e d'Oxum: In this City Everyone is Oxum's in Murphy, Joseph M. and Mei-Mei Sanford, eds. *Osun Across the Waters: A Yoruba Goddess in Africa on the Americas*. Indiana: Indiana University Press.

Roberts, June E.
    2006 *Reading Erna Brodber Uniting the Black Diaspora through Folk Culture and Religion*. Westport, CT: Praeger Publishers.

Ross, Bruce
    1996 "The Dark, Fearful Bush: Loss and Restoration in Amos Tutuola's The Palm-Wine Drinkard" in *And the Bird Began to Sing: Religion and Literature in Post-Colonial*, edited by Jamie S. Scott. The Netherlands, Amsterdam: Editions Podopi B. V.

Sargent, Sophia Rebecca
    2003 *The Ultimate Guide to Goddess Empowerment.* Kansas City, Missouri: Andrew McMeel Publishing

Scott, Rebecca
    1988 "Brazilian Abolition in Comparative Perspective" in *Abolition of Slavery and the Aftermath of Emancipation in Brazil.* Durham, NC: Duke University Press.

Simpson, George Eaton
    1960 "Culture Change and Reintegration Found in the Cults of West Kingston, Jamaica" in Wallace, Anthony F. C. *Men and Cultures: Selected Papers.* Pennsylvania: University of Pennsylvania Press.
    1970 *Religious Cults of the Caribbean: Trinidad, Jamaica, and Haiti.* Rio Piedras, Institute of the Caribbean Studies: University of Puerto Rico.

Smith, E. ed.
    1950 *African Ideas of God.* London: Edinburgh Press.

Smythe, Hugh H and Mabel M.
    1961 *The Nigerian Elite.* Palo Alto, California: Stanford University Press.

Stephen S. Farrow
    1996 *Faith, Fancies, and Fetish*: Athelia Henrietta Press, INC.

Stevenson, Carmen
    2001 *The Oracle: The Voice of Visionary Poetry.* Lincoln, NE: Writers Club Press.

Tate, Karen
    2006 *Sacred Places of Goddess 108 Destinations.* San Francisco: Consortium of Collective Consciousness Publishing.

Taylor, Nya Kwiawon Sr.
    1984 *Impact of the African Tradition on African Christianity.* Chicago, Illinois: The Strugglers' Community Press.

Taylor, John V.
    1963, 1964 *The Primal Vision: Christian Presence Amid African Religion.* London: S. M. C. Press; Philadelphia: Fortress Press.

Teish, Luisah
    2000 *Jump Up – Good Times Throughout the Seasons with Celebrations from Around the World.* Berkley, California: Conari Press.

Thorpe, S. A.
    1991 *African Traditional Religions.* Pretoria: University of South Africa.

Turner, H. W.
    1967 *African Independent Church: The Life and Faith of Church of the Lord (Aladura).* London: Oxford Press.

Uka, E. M. ed.
    1991 *Readings in African Traditional Religion Structure, Meaning, Relevance, Future.* Bern: Peter Lang.

Vale de Almeida, Miguel
    2004 *An Earth-Colored Sea: "Race" Culture, and the Politics of Identity in the Post-Colonial Portuguese-Speaking World.* Oxford, NY: Berghahn Books.

Vansina, Jan
    2006 *Oral Tradition: a Study in Historical Methodology.* Translated from French by H. M. Wright. New Brunswick, New Jersey: Aldine Transaction.

Vansina, Jan
    1985 *Oral Tradition as History.* Madison, Wisconsin: University of Wisconsin Press.

Verger, Pierre
    1976 *Trade Relations Between the Bight of Benin and Bahia from the 17th to 19th Century*. Translated by Evelyn Crawford. Ibadan, Nigeria: Ibadan University Press.

Waldherr, Kris
    2007 *Goddess Inspiration Oracle Guide*. Woodbury, MN: Llewelly Worldwide.

Wahlman, Maude Southwell
    2001 "African Charm Tradition" in *Self-Taught Art: The Culture and Aesthics of American Vernacular Art*. Mississippi: University of Mississippi.

Walker, Steven F
    2002 *The Jung and the Jungians on Myth: an Introduction on Myth*. NY & London: Routledge.

Wallace, Anthony F. C.
    1960 *Men and Cultures: Selected Papers*. Pennsylvania: University of Pennsylvania Press.

Warner-Lewis, Maureen
    1999 "The Diaspora: Orientations and Determinations" in Okpewho, Isidore, Carol Boyce Davies, Ali A. Mazuri, eds. *African Origins and New World Identities*. Bloomington: Indiana University.

Wafer, Jim William
    1991 *The Taste of Blood: Spirit Possession in Brazilian Candomble*. Pennsylvanian Press

Webster, James Bertin
    1964 *The African Churches Among the Yoruba, 1881-1922*. Oxford: Clarendon Press.

Wenger, Susanne
    1977 *The Timeless Mind of the Sacred: Its New Manifestation in the Osun Groves*. Ibadan: Institutes of African Studies, University of Ibadan.

Wishart, Catherine
    2003 *Teen Goddess: How to Look, Love and Live Like a Goddess*. St. Paul, MN: Llewellyn Worldwide.

Zahan, Dominique
    1970 *The Religion, Spirituality, and Thought of Traditional Africa*. Chicago: University of Chicago Press.

Journal Articles

Abimbola, Wande
    1975 "Yoruba Oral Tradition" Ile-Ife, Nigeria: Department of African Languages and Literatures, University of Ile, 1975: 157-197.
    1994 "Gods Versus Anti-Gods: Conflict and Resolution in the Yoruba Cosmos." *Dialogue and Alliance: Journal of the International Religious Foundation* 8 Fall/Winter, 1994: 75-87. .

Adeboye Babalola,
    1964 "The Characteristic Features of Outer form of Yoruba Ijala Chants Part II." 1 number 2 *Odu*, January 1965 Institute of African Studies, University of Ife, 1964, 47.

Adedeji, J. A.
    1967 "Form and Function of Satire in Yoruba Drama," 4 number 1 July 1967: 61-67.

1971 "Oral tradition and the Contemporary Theater in Nigeria," *Research in African Literatures* 2 no. 2 Fall 1971: 135.

Babatunde Lawal,
  1974 "Some Aspects of Yoruba Aesthetics" *British Journal of Aesthetics* 14 number 3 Summer 1974: 239-243.

Bamgbose, Ayo
  1968 "The Form of Yoruba Proverbs" 4 number 2 (January 1968): 73-86.

Bascom, William R.
  1942 "The Principle of Seniority in the Social Structure of the Yoruba" *American Anthropologist,* New Series 44 (January-March, 1942): 37-42.
  1943 "The Relationship of Yoruba Folklore to Divining" *Journal of American Folklore* (January-March, 1943): 127-131.
  1944 "The Sociological Role of the Yoruba Cult-Group," *American Anthropologist New Series* 46 January 1944: 1 Part 2.
  1967 *African Arts Catalogue* (April 6 / October 22, 1967): 1

Beier, Ulli
  1962 Nigerian Folk Art," *Nigeria Magazine* December 1962: 26-32.
  1972 "Preservation and Protection of Nigerian Antiquities," *African Notes: Bulletin of the Institutes of African Studies.* Report of a symposium held at the Institute of African Studies, University of Ibadan from Thursday 20th April to Sunday
    23rd April, 1972.

Berger, Peter L.
  1967 *The Sacred Canopy: Elements of a Sociological Theory of Religion.* Garden City, NY.: Anchor Books, 1967.

Canon, Walter B.
  1942 "Voodoo Death" *American Anthropologist.* New Series 44 number 2 April-June, 1942: 169-181.

Clark, J. P.
  1966 "Some Aspects of Nigeria Drama," *Nigeria Magazine* June 1966: 119.

De Graft, J. C.
  1976 "Roots of African Drama and Theatre," *African Literature Today* 8 (1976):1-25.

Drewal, H. J.
  "Performing the Other: Mami Wata Worship in Africa" in *The Drama Review* 32: 160-185.

Fotos de Pierre Verger
  1985 *From Slave Quarters to Town Houses.* Sao Paulo, Brazil: Impresso no Brasil.

Glazier, Stephen D.
  1996 "New World African Ritual: Genuine and Spurious" *Journal for the Scientific Study of Religion* volume 35 December 1996: 420-31.

Greene, Sandra
  1996 "Religion, History and the Supreme Gods of Africa: A Contribution to the Debate," *Journal of Religion in Africa* XXVI, 2: 1996: 115-136

Hackett, Rosalind I. J.
  1988 "The Academic Study of Religion in Nigeria", in *Religion* 18 (1988): 1:37-46.

Herskovits
  "Some Next Steps in the Study of Negro Folklore," *Journal of American Folklore* 56 no. 219.

Klein, Martin A.
1978 "The Study of Slavery in Africa" *Journal of African History,* XX, I (1978): 599-609
Lawal,
1974 "Some Aspects of Yoruba Aesthetics" *British Journal of Aesthetics* 14 number 3 (Summer 1974): 239-243.
Marie-Theresa Brincard
1985 "Beauty by Design: the Aesthetics of African Adornment"
African Studies Center, University of California XIX number 1(November 1985): 23-25.
Mckenzie, P. R.
1976 "Yoruba *Orisa* Cults: Some Marginal Notes Concerning their Cosmology and Concepts of Deity," *Journal of Religion in Africa. Religion en Afrique* 8 no. 3 (1976): 197-199.
Odera Oruka, H.
1983 "Historical Phases" *International Philosophical Quarterly* XXIII number 4 issue number 93 (December 1983): 384-392.
Ojo, J. R.
1979 "Semiotic Elements in Yoruba and Ritual," *Journal of the International Association fro Semiotic Studies* 28-3/4 (1979): 334.
Olabimtan, Afolabi
1974 "Spiritual Hierarchy in Yoruba Traditional Religion." *Journal of Religious Thought* 31 no. 1 (1974): 44 -58.
Olugunna, Deji
1959 *Osogbo, the Origin, Growth and Problems.* Oshogbo, Nigeria: Fad's Print Works.
Omoyajowo, J. Akin
1975 "Concept of Man in Africa." *Orita* 9 no. 1 (1975): 34-47.
Onyewuenyi, Innocent
1984 "Traditional African Aesthetics: A Philosophical Perspective" *International Philosophical Quarterly* XXIV number 3, Issue 95 (September 1984), 242
Oyekan Owomoyela
1971 "Folklore and Yoruba Theatre," *Research in African Literatures* 2 no. 2 (Fall 1971):123-275.
Peel, John
1967 "Religious Change in Yorubaland." *Africa* 37, no. 3. (1967): 292-306.
Schiltz, Marc
1985 Yoruba Thunder Deities and Sovereignty: Ara versus Sango." *Anthropos* 80 (1985): 67-84.
Shango Festival at Oshogbo 40 (1953)
Turner, H. W.
"The Way Forward in the Religious Study of African Primal Religions, in *Journal of Religion in Africa* 12, 2:1-5.
Vansina, J.
1960 "Recording the Oral History" *Journal of African History* 1 (1960):43-52.

www.ingramcontent.com/pod-product-compliance
Lightning Source LLC
Chambersburg PA
CBHW071437150426
43191CB00008B/1158